I0138558

The Journey Of Lent

Spring Training In The Faith

Daily Reflections

Richard Gribble, C.S.C.

CSS Publishing Company, Inc.
Lima, Ohio

THE JOURNEY OF LENT

Copyright © 1995 by
CSS Publishing Company, Inc.
Lima, Ohio

Library of Congress Cataloging-in-Publication Data

Gribble, Richard.
    The journey of Lent : spring training in the faith / Richard E. Gribble.
      p.   cm.
    ISBN 0-7880-0315-1
    1. Lent — Prayer-books and devotions — English. 2. Catholic Church—Prayer-books and devotions — English. I. Title.
BX2170.L4G73   1995
242'.34—dc20
                                   94-37763
                                       CIP

This book is available in the following formats, listed by ISBN:
0-7880-0315-1 Book

PRINTED IN U.S.A.

Dedication

The spirituality of an individual grows in both simple and profound ways. Although I have been privileged to find God in many things, it is certainly within humans that God's presence is most manifest to me. Many people have guided me along the spiritual journey of life, but some have been more influential. This book is dedicated to those who have helped me most along that road: My spiritual directors — Mary Ann Donovan, S.C.; Nancy Wellmeier, S.N.D. de.N.; and Margaret Mullin, S.A.; and a special friend, Mary, whose encouragement and constant care daily allows me to do my best to walk in God's way.

Table Of Contents

Introduction

The season of Lent is a special time when Christians make an extra effort to ready themselves for the Paschal mystery of Jesus' passion, death and resurrection which is celebrated in the Easter Triduum. It is a time of preparation given us by the Church to shake off the lethargy which sometimes creeps into our lifestyle and renew again our commitment to the Christian way of life. Lent is a time to get in shape for future events; it is our "spring training" in the Faith.

From the tradition of the Church we have certain areas that are annually given some emphasis in this Lenten time of preparation. We think especially of the concepts of fasting, prayer and almsgiving. The Church asks us to reflect upon these virtues and to see where we can improve or make a greater contribution. One way that the Church helps us in this quest for greater perfection, in imitation of Jesus, is through the readings chosen for daily Mass found in the lectionary. Many of the aspects of fasting, prayer and almsgiving are seen in the six-week journey of faith which is Lent.

This book is a collection of reflections based on the readings of the Lenten season. Some of the readings speak very clearly of the traditional Lenten virtues; others guide us in different aspects of the Christian life that we are called to live through our baptism. It is my hope that these reflections will serve to aid you along the path which the Lenten journey lays out for us all. Certainly some of the readings themselves will speak more forcefully to one person than another. Thus, the message of the reflection will work in a similar manner. Taken as a whole the reflections of this book aim to guide one's own meditations on God's word.

God's word must be an essential part of the Lenten journey and, therefore, our "spring training." The reflections offered for each day can best be understood and be most beneficial if they are read in conjunction with the readings for the day. It is hoped that the reader will read God's word and then use the reflection as a guide to his/her own thought and prayer.

The relationship we each share with God is without question highly personal. The reflections shared in this effort were born out of my personal relationship with God. I hope they are fruitful to you as together we walk the path toward God, our "spring training" in the faith.

Richard Gribble, CSC

Reflections:
Week Of Ash Wednesday

Ash Wednesday
Joel 2:12-18
2 Corinthians 5:20—6:2
Matthew 6:1-6, 16-18

Spring Training

As all those who follow baseball know, this is the time of spring training. Although in many areas of the country it is snowing and bitter cold still lingers, in Florida, Arizona and California the best baseball players in the country are working hard to prepare themselves for the coming season. All the players come to their respective training camps with one goal in mind — to make it to the World Series in October. The pain, the sweat, the hard work that is involved in being a baseball player is all worth it, if the goal can be accomplished.

Baseball players have to prepare themselves in at least three ways. First, they have to get into shape. Running, exercising, dieting — all may be necessary to drop extra weight and obtain the stamina that will be necessary for the long season ahead. A player who is in good shape stands a much better chance of helping his team reach that World Series goal. Next, a player needs to practice the fundamentals of the game. Constant work in the batting cage will hone the offensive skills needed to score runs. Endless hours in the field shagging flies and fielding ground balls will develop the defensive skills needed to win. Lastly, a good baseball player must develop a positive mental attitude in order to succeed. Baseball is a team game in which individuals can shine — but it is the team that wins or loses. A winning team must have a winning attitude.

The season of Lent is much like spring training in base-ball. This is a time given to us by the Church to prepare ourselves. We prepare for a goal and we need to hone our skills to succeed. Our readings today describe what the goal is and what we need to do to achieve it.

The goal for all Christians is not difficult to determine. The prophet Joel speaks God's word and says, "Return to me with your whole heart, ... rend your hearts and not your garments, and return to the Lord, your God." There is no magic or new revelation here. God desires that we return to our creator, the one from whom we came in the beginning. We are to be reconciled to God, as St. Paul says in the Second Reading, so we might become the very holiness of God.

How do we return to God; how can we be reconciled to the Lord? The Gospel today describes the three traditional Lenten means to prepare ourselves for the return journey. First, Jesus says we need to be almsgivers. Sharing the gifts of God which may be ours is part of the Christian call which this holy season asks of us. We need to spend some time in reflection as to what that might mean for us this year. Possibly it will mean giving of our resources to some project or fund. It might mean that our very valuable time will be given to others so that their life may be bettered.

Next, Jesus says we need to pray. We know that we always need to pray, but today we are called to a renewal in our prayer life. Maybe this rethinking will manifest itself in more quiet time with God; possibly it is an invitation to a new form of prayer. The challenge is to make certain that we spend sufficient time with our God.

Thirdly, Jesus suggests that we need to fast. Catholics have special "fast" days built into the liturgical calendar, like today and Good Friday. Catholics are asked to refrain from eating meat on Fridays. While Protestants have no fast days as such, fasting can be so much more if we try. If we give up some food item, if we choose to skip a couple of meals per week — can we then spend the time and/or the resources that would have been expended in eating in some activity of additional prayer or ministry? The greatest challenge of all may be to practice the traditional Lenten observances with a new attitude that says I am preparing myself for God in a special and meaningful way and not, as the Gospel describes, so that others may see what we do.

Lent is here and our preparation must begin. Athletes, as St. Paul once wrote, deny themselves many things to win a crown of laurel — we might say a World Series ring. But Christians during Lent deny themselves so as to prepare for the Easter event, a mystery of untold significance. Let us today think about our own preparation, our own "spring training," so that we can return to God, be reconciled, and find eternal life.

Thursday After Ash Wednesday
Deuteronomy 30:15-20
Luke 9:22-25

The
Christian Paradox

If you look in a dictionary for the word "paradox" you will find a definition which in paraphrased form would say: a statement that on first inspection appears to be false, but on closer examination is found to be true. There are many examples of paradoxes in our world. I can think of two, one in literature and one in mathematics. The famous dialogue "Meno" by Plato contains a well-known paradox. In the dialogue Socrates is speaking with his friend Meno. In the course of their lively exchange Meno poses the question, "Is it possible to know that which is not learned?" Meno's answer is a resounding no — there is nothing that a human being knows that has not been learned. Socrates, however, says the answer is yes; it is a paradox. There are certain things, such as the emotions of love, that a human knows without being taught; they are innate to the human psyche.

Another paradox comes from the world of numbers. If you want to get from point A to point B, and each time you move you travel exactly one-half of the remaining distance between where you are and the intended goal, how long will it take you to arrive? One might initially answer, "This cannot be that hard; I must be able to calculate the answer!" Actually, however, the answer is that you will never arrive at the desired destination. You will come infinitesimally close, but never arrive, for you can go only one-half of the remaining distance with each move. It is a paradox.

Certainly the greatest of all paradoxes is that of Christianity itself. We hear about that paradox in today's Gospel. Jesus says that in order to save your life you must lose it. This, of course, makes no sense to the initial hearing. That is why St. Paul referred to the cross as an absurdity to those who do not believe. Jesus says that it is only in dying to self that we are able to find eternal life with God. There appears to be another paradox, or at least a contradiction, in today's readings as well. Moses in the first reading tells the people to choose life over death. When we look at the context and the overall message of Moses, however, we will see that the liberator of the Hebrews from bondage in Egypt is saying that the people need to choose life for others. Thus, there is not a contradiction, but rather, a correlation in today's readings. Both tell us that we need to live for others so as to find God.

We have a choice from God's gift of free will. We can choose life for ourselves. On the surface this seems to be the only logical way to go. It is the only path by which we can find that which society says is so important, even vital, the material things of this world. But the paradox is that this path, although appealing and usually less congested and trouble-free, will, in the end, lead nowhere. The only way that leads to life, eternal life with God, is to live for others. As the Gospel says, we need to daily pick up our cross and follow in the way of the Lord. It may not be easy, but then Jesus never promised any of his followers a path swept clean of pain, troubles and other hazards.

As our Lenten journey begins let us choose life for others. The ways will vary; the methods will be diverse. Yet, the result will be the same: life with Jesus, who is brother, friend and Lord to us all.

Friday After Ash Wednesday
Isaiah 58:1-9
Matthew 9:14-15

Welcoming Others

On December 8, 1932, a young woman reporter on assignment for *America* magazine came to Washington, D.C. She came to cover a protest march to be held that day. After covering her story, she came to the Shrine of the Immaculate Conception on the campus of the Catholic University of America. As a recent convert to Catholicism she came to this church on its special feast day to attend Mass. While there she prayed fervently to God that she would be shown a new direction in life. Her past had been painful including a broken marriage and an abortion. She asked God to direct her to the vocation which had been planned for her. She left the Shrine that day confident that God would answer her prayer.

When she returned to her small, lower eastside Manhattan apartment she soon realized that she would not have long to wait to hear God's answer to her prayer. Friends told her that a man had been asking for her in her absence. He insisted upon staying in the apartment until he could speak with her. This man, a French immigrant to the United States via Canada, had a new vision of life. He wanted to give back to all people the Christian dignity which was theirs from God. His plan included houses of hospitality to shelter those who needed a home and farming communes to emphasize the "return to the land" mentality which was popular in those days. Finally, his plan included the need for lively discussions in which the problems of society could be properly addressed and solutions found. His plan needed someone to organize it and bring it to reality. Thus, on that day the man with an idea, Peter Maurin, and the woman of organization and journalism, Dorothy Day, formed a partnership which would become the Catholic Worker Movement, publishing its first one cent monthly paper on May 1, 1933. The *Catholic Worker* is a ministry of help; it reaches out to serve the poor, neglected and fringe peoples of our society. At its heart, however, the movement is a ministry of welcome for those whom society has discarded as useless or unproductive.

I am sure Dorothy Day and Peter Maurin wore big smiles when they read the words of Isaiah contained in today's First Reading. We know that Lent is a time of fasting, a time to give up something so as to prepare ourselves — spring training as we said. Fasting in this way is good, holy and welcomed by God. But Isaiah is suggesting that there may be another form of fasting that is equally important and has an active element to it. This is the fasting we hear described by the prophet. He says God desires a fast which gives release to those unjustly bound, setting free the oppressed, feeding the hungry, sheltering the homeless and clothing the naked. These acts of kindness will produce a light which will break forth like the dawn. All of these acts as well describe the ministry of welcome to those whom society has forgotten.

Jesus also speaks of welcome in today's Gospel. The disciples of John the Baptist want to know why Jesus' apostles do not fast. Jesus, simply put, says that as long as he, the groom, is with them the apostles cannot fast. No, they have a more active apostolate to engage — that of welcoming the Jews and those on the outside into the life and ministry of Jesus. It requires energy — thus, the disciples cannot fast.

The ministry of welcome is an often overlooked aspect of our Christian call. Each day we have opportunities to give welcome to others. It may be a member of our family, a friend or a business associate. We may be called upon to offer welcome to the lowly, the *anawim* of this world. It just might

17

be as well that a more fervent welcome needs to be extended to God in our lives.

We have many examples of welcome in today's Mass. We have the example of Dorothy Day and Peter Maurin; we have the words of Isaiah and the challenge of Jesus. Let us be more welcoming in all that we do, so that in the end God will welcome us as well.

Saturday After Ash Wednesday
Isaiah 58:9-14
Luke 5:27-32

The Lenten Check-Up

There is a popular expression which says, "If it ain't broke, don't fix it." Some people use this attitude in the way they use cars, their homes and especially systems of operation and ways of doing things. For some items this may be the best policy, but probably not for all things. There is another attitude that says we must periodically make checks on things to see that they are still properly functioning. During my time in the Navy we used a system called Planned Maintenance System or PMS for short. This system required a periodic maintenance on every piece of equipment on our ship. Some checks were done weekly; others were conducted monthly, quarterly or after a prescribed amount of running time. We can see a similar idea when we change the oil in our car every 3,000 miles or rotate the tires at 5,000-mile intervals We could all think of different things in our lives that we periodically check to see their condition and ability to operate properly.

The readings today seem to take the second of our two possible attitudes with respect to the check-up which we must make on our spiritual lives. We are encouraged to be active and do something today, not to wait until something goes wrong. Continuing from yesterday's First Reading Isaiah today again tells us that a light will rise if we feed the hungry and satisfy the afflicted. The prophet says further that if we will allow God to act then our strength will be renewed like a watered garden or a spring whose source of water never ends. When we act we are challenged to act for God and God's people, not for ourselves. In short, we need to look after our sisters and brothers at all times, not only when they call upon us.

The Gospel also speaks of the active ministry. Jesus suggests that we must reach out to those who are damaged, broken or incomplete. In his own life Jesus came to call sinners, not those who have no need for a doctor. Jesus will not wait until we think we need him; he is there now and always will be inviting us to participate more fully in his life today. The call by Jesus of the tax collector Levi, a stereotypical sinner in the eyes of the Jews, is the example which Jesus gives us in searching out the lost. Active ministry does not wait for humans to fail; it seeks to aid people all along the road of life.

Jesus, the great healer, came to heal us. Jesus came to save us from the evils and pitfalls of this world, and even at times from ourselves. Lent is a time to check up on ourselves, to make an annual evaluation and inspection. How are we doing in our Christian life? How have we been doing in our life of discipleship? What is the status of our ministry to our sisters and brothers who are in need? Why do we do what we do; what is our attitude? Do we do things for self or for God and God's people?

Let us during this Lenten journey take ourselves in for our annual check-up with the great healer, Jesus, the Lord. If we can be truthful in our self-examination through prayer and reflection, then certainly as Isaiah says, the light will shine, we will ride on the heights of the earth and our preparation will be that much better for the great Easter event.

Reflections:
Week One Of Lent

Monday Week One
Leviticus 19:1-2, 11-18
Matthew 25:31-46

Be Holy
As Is God

We all know that God is divine. This is how we define God.
But how does one define divinity? One might say that divinity means omniscience and omnipotence. These are both proper
descriptions, possibly even definitions of divinity, but how can
a human relate to these things? We know so many things that
are more powerful than we and so many people who are more
intelligent than ourselves. Maybe we can imagine the divinity
of God as all love or all compassion. I think this gets us
closer for we can relate better to this understanding of God.
We have all loved and been loved. We all try to show compassion.

The best definition I have ever heard for divinity, at least
the one that seems to make sense and in which I can participate is this: to the extent that I am able to live for others is
the degree in which I participate in the divinity which is God.

Our readings today speak about living for others as the way
that leads to God, and thereby to God's divinity. The book
of Leviticus, from which our first reading is drawn, is a book
of laws. For most of us today when we think of the law we
think of restrictions. We hear of all the things that the law
does not allow and we think that a straightjacket has been
placed around us. Laws, however, are only restrictive to those
who want to get away with more than is actually theirs in the
first place. Laws order our lives and keep us from living in

chaos. Imagine driving on the highways with no laws. The Law for the Hebrew people was a way of life. It was their method of finding God. The Law was a path which if followed would lead one to a more full and complete life in God's presence. In the reading God tells Moses that it is in caring for others that we find God. God says we are not to defraud, to be just to the weak and the strong. We are to make no judgments; we are to cast aside hatred and revenge. In short, we are to love our neighbor as ourself, the same exhortation we heard in last week's readings.

The Gospel story of the end times, what is known as eschatological literature, is familiar to all of us. Jesus says that when we do things for others, especially the least of our sisters and brothers, we do it for him. When we are compassionate, when we share and visit others, then we find God and participate in the divinity which is God. When we find God in this life we have the promise of eternal life as well. On the other hand if we neglect to be present to others, to feed, clothe or visit them, then we have neglected God as well. Such inattention will lead to eternal condemnation.

Lent challenges us with renewal in all aspects of our lives. We are asked this day to reflect upon the opportunities which God gives us to live for others and, thereby, to share in God's divinity. The opportunity today might be helping someone who needs you; it may be a visit to a sick neighbor. The opportunity today may be merely a kind word offered at the right moment. Let us look for the opportunities that God provides this day. Let us see them as a path to life. Let us serve others. Let us be holy as God is Holy.

Tuesday Week One
Isaiah 55:10-11
Matthew 6:7-15

Prayer
Nourishes Us

Anyone who has ever tended a garden, whether it be vegetables, flowers or other plants, can understand the need for water. Water is life sustaining to plants; without water plants wither and die. The water which ultimately comes from the heavens sinks down deep into the soil. It gives nourishment to the roots which supply the needs for the whole plant. The water has a distinct purpose; water gives life. The same need that plants have for water is present with humans. We use water in drinking, cooking, cleaning and even transportation through the great rivers and oceans of our world. Ancient civilizations knew the importance, the absolute necessity, of water as well as we do today.

The imagery of Isaiah in today's First Reading is alive for all of us, even if we live in the concrete jungle of the city. The water, we are told, will not return to the clouds until it serves its purpose. We know this is true from our own experience in working with or observing plants. In a similar way God's word is like the rain and snow that come from the heavens; they will not return until they too accomplish their purpose. It might seem today, in a world which appears on the surface to care little for God or God's message of peace, that the word of God is not accomplishing the purpose for which it was given to our world. This is only the surface appearance, however. Talk sometime with a person who works with prisoners or with the poor. You will find in their reflections on life and ministry plenty of genuine stories of faith and conversion. People continue each day to hear the word of God, be moved to action, and in the process serve the needs of God and God's people. God's word continues to be as effective and as challenging as the two-edged sword metaphor used by the author of the Letter to the Hebrews in describing God's word.

God's word for us can be best seen in prayer. Today's Gospel gives us the most complete and yet simple prayer we can possibly find. The Lord's Prayer is the only one which Jesus taught his disciples and thus it has immense significance for those of us who follow in the Fisherman's footsteps. In this prayer, a reflection of God's word, we ask for our daily needs. We also ask to be forgiven as we forgive others. For God's word to be effective, for it to water and nourish us, as it was intended to do, we must be open to a change of heart. We must be willing to forgive and be forgiven. In short, the Lenten season calls us to be a reconciliation people. Reconciliation begins with self, moves to others and finds its ultimate fulfillment in our pursuit and discovery of God. It is up to us, however, to pursue reconciliation and make it a reality in our lives.

Today as we live in God's presence, let us allow God's word to water and feed us as the rains and snow water the land and its produce. Let God's word penetrate us. Let us be strengthened by God's word for the Lenten journey ahead!

Wednesday Week One
Jonah 3:1-10
Luke 11:29-32

The Courage
To Change

Change is something we all experience, whether we like it or not. Change is all about us. The weather changes from day to day and we have absolutely no control over it. Fashion changes from season to season. One year it is wide ties and pump shoes and the next it is narrower ties and loafers. Changes exist even in the Church. We move from the white of the Christmas season, to the green of ordinary time, to the purple of the present season of Lent. The Gospel acclamation is changed in Lent and the Gloria is not prayed. The tone of celebration is more somber and reflective.

Are you a person who welcomes change or resists it? Some people like change for change's sake. They see it as exciting, even necessary, to keep things in perspective. Other people are highly resistant to change. They see change as too risky and challenging, or simply too much trouble.

What does it take for you to change? What changes are possible for you? Changing the externals is usually acceptable to most — it is not threatening. We can change our outward appearance through hairstyle or clothes, we can rearrange the furniture in our home, we can even shuffle the worship space in our churches and few, if any, seem to be offended. These changes are transitory; they are not permanent. Maybe this is why they are easier to accept. A fashion consultant, interior decorator or Church liturgist can effect change and most remain calm and unflustered.

27

What about change on the inside, in our hearts? Here the change is more difficult. Such changes cannot be seen, yet they are permanent. They are filled with risk because we know that something basic to who or what we are will necessitate some alteration. Our fear leads to hesitation toward or even rejection of such change.

Our readings today talk about change. They refer to the latter type of change, on the inside. We are given two different reactions to change as well as two different people as signs of the need to change. The Ninevites, from what we know in the Hebrew Scriptures, were a rebellious and sinful people. They lived for the day; they refused to seek God. Yet, they are told to change their whole lives, their thoughts, their hearts. They are asked to change on the inside and they do it without hesitation. Jonah can only make it through one-third of the city, and all are converted.

Jesus came to another people at a later time. They too were sinful in Jesus' description of this as an evil age. The people of Jesus' day as well needed to reform, to change on the inside, but they refused. The people had the preaching of Jesus as a sign, one much greater than Jonah, but they still refused to listen and heed the warning of God. Because of their rejection of Jesus' message, it is the people of Nineveh who will condemn them.

What about us — what sign, what person or event do we need in order to change? Sociologists say that our basic social and moral values are "locked-in" by age 18. In order to change we need to experience a "significant emotional event" or S.E.E. in our lives, such as a death in the family, loss of job, divorce or some type of physical or mental incapacitation. I am not sure, however, if the sociologists promoting the need for an S.E.E. realized the power of faith and belief in God, and its ability to change people. We have the opportunity during this season to reverse the trend we hear related in today's readings. The Ninevites changed but the Jews refused. The Ninevites had a prophet, Jonah. The Jews had a greater prophet, Jesus the Christ. With faith we too can change.

We do not have Jesus' physical presence with us, but we have more than enough signs. We know more than the Jews did. We know about Jonah and the physical life of Jesus, as did the Jews. But we also know the end of the Gospel story, the passion, death and resurrection of Jesus. We are benefactors of 2,000 years of Christian tradition. Lent is a time when reflection on change and transformation in our lives is encouraged. What change of heart or mind do we need? What new direction is Jesus suggesting to us this day through our conversation with him? We must understand that we have the tradition; we have the signs. Let us endeavor to change as God suggests to each of us in our daily walk of prayer. Let us be transformed by God this day!

Thursday Week One
Esther (C) 4:12, 14-16, 23-25
Matthew 7:7-12

Trust Fully
In God

Albert Schweitzer is a name familiar to most all. He gained
fame as a medical missionary in Africa in the early 20th century. This, however, is only the end of a larger story. Schweitzer
answered several calls in his life, all invitations from God. He
responded to all, confident that God would be with him.

Born to a Lutheran pastor and his wife it was natural for
young Albert to pursue theological study. He received doc-
torates in both theology and philosophy. In the early 1900s
he wrote a book describing the *Quest For The Historical Jesus*.
The book, almost overnight, made Schweitzer a respected
member of the theological intelligentsia.

Such fame and possibilities for the future did not deter
Schweitzer from following other invitations extended by God.
From youth Albert had been blessed with the gift of musical
ability. He became one of the premier organists in all Europe
and is still considered, even in this age of CDs and laser discs,
as one of the foremost interpreters who ever lived of Bach's
music.

God was not through with Albert Schweitzer, however; there
was one more invitation to be extended. At the height of his
fame as both a theologian and, in his spare time, a musician,
Schweitzer answered God's call to go to the African missions
as a doctor. He received his medical training and promptly set
up a mission clinic to meet the needs not only of the local

community, but to serve as a regional facility for the treatment of leprosy. For his efforts he was awarded the Nobel Peace Prize in 1952 on behalf of "The Brotherhood of Nations."

Albert Schweitzer's life is a good example of what our readings tell us today — we need to trust completely in God. The book of Esther speaks of the plot to have all Jews, then in captivity in Babylon, slaughtered out of the treachery of Haman. Esther, as we hear in today's reading, cries to God about the plot she has discovered. She places all of her trust and confidence in God. God alone is her help and the only hope of her people as well. Esther realizes that God alone can save her.

In the Gospel today Jesus speaks of God as a father who gives his children all that they need. God can only give good things. Jesus knows that good parents want to help their children; it is the right thing to do. Better than the best parent, however, is the love that God will show to all his children. As Jesus says, those who ask will receive, those who seek will find, and those who knock will be granted entrance.

Where do we place our trust? In whom or what do we place our hope? The quick fix is the answer for some. This is the bandaid approach. We find temporary solace in someone or something. We find comfort, we may even be raised to new heights, but only for a limited amount of time. In the end such solutions resolve nothing. Some seek permanent solutions to life's difficulties in human remedies. These are more tangible, even visible. Thus, they seem to be more real and filled with more answers.

The only true solution, however, can be found in God. In the daily walk of our life we need to be open, to allow God to guide us, most especially when we think all is well and we know the way. If we allow God to light our way through the darkness and even the brightness of life, we will find the ultimate answers to life's quest, peace with God and self. For as the Gospel says, God will give only good things to those who ask. Let us open ourselves during this Lenten journey, as did Albert Schweitzer, to the possibilities of God. Let us place our lives totally in the hands of God.

Friday Week One
Ezekiel 18:21-28
Matthew 5:20-26

Return To
The Lord

The name of John Newton is probably not familiar to many, even those in the world of music. But the one song with which he is associated through its composition, "Amazing Grace," has in many ways immortalized him. The song and its words are familiar to all Christians; it certainly is one of the most popular hymns ever written. The words of "Amazing Grace" are autobiographical; they tell a story of conversion and return to the Lord.

John Newton was the son of a sea-going Englishman and his wife. It was quite natural for Newton to follow in his father's footsteps. Newton was apprenticed on cargo ships as a deck hand. On one voyage from Europe to America a violent storm almost caused the vessel to sink. Newton, who although baptized had never practiced Christianity, saw in his survival the sign that he needed to turn his life around. He began to attend Episcopal services, but he still was not converted.

His life with the sea continued in a new and more cruel way as he became the captain of a slave trading vessel. For six years Newton ferried slaves from Africa to the American continent. Over time he became horrified at the whole slave concept and later in life campaigned against it as one of the first of what later became known as the abolitionist movement. Leaving the sea for good, Newton began to study for the ministry and eventually served as an Episcopal priest. The words of his famous song, "I once was lost but now am found, was blind but now I see," tell the story of the conversion of Newton from a life of sin to one of service.

Our readings today speak of the concept of conversion and how God rejoices over our ability to be reconciled with one another. The prophet Ezekiel says that God is desirous that we become transformed to a life of virtue and rid ourselves of all that draws us away from God. The final aspect of our life is what counts; we need to put on the Lord and refuse to be mystified by the evilness that surrounds us. God will rejoice if we can find conversion in our life.

In the Gospel we hear a passage on reconciliation, but one that at first reading might sound confusing. We are all familiar with many examples in the Scriptures where Jesus is seemingly quite lenient in his attitude toward the sinner. There are several examples of how Jesus defends the disciples (or even Himself) when they break the sabbath law. We know well the story of the woman caught in adultery and how Jesus shows no condemnation. Jesus even forgave those who participated in his agonizing and shameful death on the cross.

Today, however, Jesus says that anger with a brother or sister, abusive language or holding others in contempt will be placed on a par with murder. It appears at first that Jesus has matched the same punishment to offenses of greatly different severity. Jesus is making a point on reconciliation. Anger and abusive language draw us away from others just as if we had murdered a person. As Jesus suggests, we need to be reconciled. We need to settle with our opponents. We need to be reunited with our brothers and sisters. This must come before we can adequately and sincerely offer our gift to God.

Reconciliation is an active virtue with an initial passive component. God welcomes us back into the divine fold with open arms at any and all times. We merely need as God's children to passively accept God's love and forgiveness. After this, however, our reconciliation becomes active. We need to seek reconciliation with others — those we may have hurt, those who may have hurt us.

As we spend this day let us think of one person with whom we need to seek reconciliation. Let us go and actively be re-united with that person. Then we can, as the Gospel suggests, seek greater unity with God, the source of all that is good.

Saturday Week One
Deuteronomy 26:16-19
Matthew 5:43-48

Look To
Higher Realms

We all know from our study of history and the catechism that we are members of the Judeo-Christian heritage. The first Christians were themselves Jews. Jesus, his mother and foster-father, and his disciples were all good practicing Jews. St. Paul describes himself as a Pharisee in his zealous practice of the Jewish tradition. The Jewish tradition of which we are all inheritors gave us many things. We have a sense of community from Judaism, as well as our monotheistic belief. Above all the Jewish tradition gave us the law of the covenant, so that we would have a rule by which to live and a promise we could all share.

Today in the first reading we hear about the heritage that is ours. Moses speaks to the people and he tells them about both the law and the covenant. The law was given by God to Moses. In its basic form we know it as the Ten Commandments. The law was expanded, as we can read in the Book of Leviticus, to an all-inclusive pattern for life. Moses also tells the people that they are uniquely God's own, a special promise from God. If the people uphold all the statutes, decrees and commandments of God, if they harken to God's voice, then they will be raised up to special heights of praise and renown. The glory of Israel will be made known to all nations.

When Jesus came the law was still the basis of all Hebrew belief. Jesus, however, asks that the people look to new heights in their life. As with yesterday's Gospel Jesus now expects more from the people. The law was good, but now Jesus asks the people, he asks us, to go further. The old law said you could love the people of your country and hate your enemies. The Lord says we need to do better — we need to love our enemies as well. In fact, Jesus suggests that there is little merit in loving those who will love us in return. We know how difficult it can be to love those who have not the desire nor it seems the ability to love us in return. Unanswered love can be quite draining, but Jesus asks us to try. Jesus in his life initiated a new covenant of love; the law could go only so far.

Lent is a time to stretch ourselves, to go beyond where we presently find ourselves. Traditionally this discipline has manifested itself in denial of things that we particularly enjoy and in which we habitually participate, whether it be some type of food or drink, recreational activity or some vice. Denial is a good form of discipline and should be practiced. Today, however, Jesus challenges us to look to new heights, new horizons in our life. How can we be better servants, better ministers to God and God's people? How can the baptismal commitment which we all possess deepen our life in the Spirit? In what ways can I go beyond that which is normally expected and reach new heights in my relationship with God?

Christianity is a challenge; it should not be easy. Challenge pushes us to seek new ways of finding God. The letter of the law may be all that is required by some, but the Lord asks us this day to consider more the spirit of the law and how we might be able to more fully participate. Let us reflect in our lives how we might be able to do more, to love more fully, to reach a new level in our relationship with God.

Reflections:
Week Two Of Lent

Monday Week Two
Daniel 9:4-10
Luke 6:36-38

The Compassion
Of God

Joseph Girzone, the popular author, tells the following story in his parable *Joshua And The Children*.[1] Over a hundred years ago in France, a butler attached to a wealthy family knew where the family kept all their money, hidden in a vault underneath their chateau. The butler methodically plotted to kill everyone in the family and steal the money. One night when everyone was asleep, he crept into the house and first murdered the father and mother. Then one by one he began to murder the children. The youngest escaped because he heard noises and could not sleep. When he realized what was happening he quietly slipped out of his bedroom and hid in a closet under a pile of clothes.

For years the boy wandered the streets as an orphan. He eventually entered the seminary and became a priest. After several years he was assigned to Devil's Island as a chaplain. One afternoon one of the convict inmates came running in from the fields, frantically calling for the chaplain. "There is a man dying out in the field, Father. Come quickly."

The priest ran out with the inmate and reached the dying prisoner. Kneeling down beside him, the priest lifted the man's head onto his lap and asked if he would like to confess his sins. The dying man refused. "Why, my son?" asked the priest. "Because God will never forgive me for what I have done."

39

"But what have you done that is so bad?" the priest continued. And the man went on to tell the story of how he had killed this whole family so that he could have their money, and only the little boy escaped because he could not find him.

Then the priest said to the dying man, "If I can forgive you then certainly God can forgive you. And I forgive you from my heart. It was my family you killed, and I am that little boy."

The convict cried and told the priest how he had been haunted all his life over what he had done, though no one else knew about it. Even the authorities never found out. The two men cried together. As the priest was giving the dying man absolution, the prisoner died with his head resting on the priest's lap.

This powerful story, which I have heard in other places and know to be true, speaks clearly of the great compassion and love which God has for us, no matter what has happened or when it occurred. God will provide the opportunity to release ourselves from the bondage that sin can sometimes bring to our lives. Our readings today speak of the magnanimous forgiveness and compassion of God for all people.

The first reading from Daniel is a great prayer. The Hebrews are in exile in Babylon. They know that they have transgressed God's law. That is why they have been placed in the hands of the Babylonians. The Hebrews have sinned and done evil in God's sight. The people are ashamed of what they have done. But the people have hope; this they never lose. The people realize that God is full of compassion and forgiveness. Although transgressions have occurred, the forgiveness of God will break through and the people will eventually be returned to their native land of Israel.

The confidence that is expressed in Daniel is manifest in the Gospel. Jesus says that we are to be compassionate and to pardon as God is compassionate and pardons us. Jesus cautions us against judgment, lest we be judged ourselves. Over all, however, Jesus says that the measure with which we measure out will be returned to us. The compassion of God will be like grain which when poured into the fold of a woman's apron runs over on all sides because it is so abundant. Possibly we can think of God's mercy as constantly filling a water glass and seeing the water run over on all sides, in all directions. God's love and mercy are like that. They cannot be contained; they go out to all people for all time.

Lent is a time when we think about our sinfulness. No one is perfect; as St. Paul says, all have sinned. But the important lesson today is to realize the unlimited love of God. The priest who could love and forgive the man who had killed his whole family is the image of God's love for us. One would not think such forgiveness is possible, but all is possible with God. God has no limits, although we constantly try to place limits on God, even on God's love. Let us this day remember the unlimited love of God and be welcomed by Jesus. His arms are open on the cross just waiting for us. As the Scriptures say, "Come inherit the kingdom prepared for you since the beginning of time."

---

1. Joseph F. Girzone, *Joshua And The Children,* (New York: Macmillan, 1989), pp. 9-10.

Tuesday Week Two
Isaiah 1:10, 16-20
Matthew 23:1-12

Conversion To Humility

Alfred Bessette was a doorman for 50 years. That does not sound very exciting. In fact, it sounds terribly boring. Yet, through such humble work and an equally humble life this man, who took the religious name of Brother André, was raised to the level of the beatified by Pope John Paul II. Brother André was a doorman at the Oratory of St. Joseph in Montreal, Canada. The simplicity with which he lived his life as a servant was only equaled by the simplicity with which he was able to perform miraculous physical cures of many who sought his assistance.

People came from all over Canada (and many from the United States) to see Brother André. They did not come to hear eloquent speeches or to see feats of bravery or courage. They came because they believed in faith that this humble, uneducated religious brother could bring them closer to God and in the process possibly effect a cure of their bodies. Over many years the number who received physical healing grew. The effect on the soul, however, was more important. Brother André's closeness to God was transferred to all who sought his assistance in any way. His ability to cure people earned him the name of the "Miracle Worker of Montreal." His saintly, rather unspectacular life has earned him a special place in the hearts of all and the special recognition within the Communion of Saints.

We hear in today's First Reading from Isaiah, "Come now, let us set things right." Lent is a time to get our house in order. It is as we said at the outset of the season our time of preparation, our spring training in the Faith. There are many things we need to get in order. Our readings today suggest what might need our attention and most especially how we should approach this period of preparation.

Isaiah gives some very specific ideas on getting our house in order. We are told to listen to God's instruction, to wash ourselves clean, to cease doing evil and to learn to do good. We are told to make justice our aim. All of this is a tall order, but we need to daily work toward these goals.

How are we to do these things? The Gospel gives us a very specific answer. Brother André was able to order the lives of many by his life of holiness. Jesus suggests in the Gospel that we too are to order our lives, to put away misdeeds, to make justice our aim, in an unassuming way. We are not to look for titles that will gain us prestige; we are not to look for the places of honor in our place of worship. In opposition to the example of the Pharisees, who said much but did little, we are to do what we do so as not to be seen or noticed. We are to be humble in what we do, in ordering our house. As Jesus says, "Whoever exalts himself will be humbled, but whoever humbles himself will be exalted."

We all like to be recognized for what we do. This is a natural human desire, even a need. Recognition will happen along the path of life, but it should not be that for which we live. The kind of recognition we should desire is that which comes from going about our business, carrying out God's plan for us, and doing it without seeking recognition. We can all think of examples of saintly people we have known or about whom we have read who have lived humbly and through that humility been recognized.

The greatest, really the only, recognition that we need is that which comes from God. If we make up our minds to set things right, as Isaiah suggests, and we do our best to do it in an unassuming way, then certainly God will see and, like

Brother André, we will be recognized. Few if any of us will find the "official" recognition of sainthood, but if we do God's will we are God's saints. Let us learn a lesson from the humble life of an uneducated doorman; let us ready ourselves in some small way as our Lenten journey continues this day.

Wednesday Week Two
Jeremiah 18:18-20
Matthew 20:17-28

Agape —
Service To All

In the mid 1960s as I recall, Joan Baez, the well-known folk singer, wrote and sang a song called, "Love Is Just A Four-Letter Word." In the lyrics to that song Ms. Baez tried to show that although the word love has only four letters and might be thought by some, because it is a small word, to be a simple concept, it is in reality a very complex idea. We all know this to be true from the experience of our daily lives.

The ancient Greeks, a very intelligent civilization, realized that love was a complicated idea. Among the many gifts which the Greeks gave to our society was the science of philosophy, the science of thought. In philosophy and in language, the Greeks used three words to describe the vast nature of love. The first word the Greeks used was *phileo*, the idea of brotherly love. This is the love which is seen between sisters and brothers, the love expressed between good friends. The second form of love is *eros*. This is romantic love, the love between one man and one woman. This type of love is pointed inward. It is a love which satisfies our own personal need. The third, and for the Greeks the highest form of love, is *agapao*, which is commonly called *agape*. This is the outward expression of love that we show in serving others, our sisters and brothers in the Lord. *Agape* does not satisfy a personal need to feel loved, but it unquestionably satisfies the Christian need to serve and be present to others.

The readings today are filled with expressions of *agape,* love for others. Jeremiah, like many of the ancient prophets, was a bit hesitant at his role. He considered himself unworthy of the task. Yet God chose him, touched his mouth, and prepared him for his mission to the Hebrew people. Jeremiah did his best, in circumstances which were many times very trying and troublesome, to carry God's word to the nation of Israel. We hear about one of those especially troubling times in the first reading. The people of Judah and citizens of Jerusalem have hatched a plot against Jeremiah in order to end his life. Jeremiah realizes the evil in the people's hearts and speaks to God asking Him to remember his service. Jeremiah has always stood before God to speak on Israel's behalf; he has been true to his call. Jeremiah has gone forth in a ministry of service; he has shown *agape* to the people whom God has given to him.

I am sure that all of us can relate to the indignation which the other ten apostles felt toward James and John, as we hear in today's Gospel. Their mother wants her sons to sit in exalted positions in the Kingdom of God. Jesus wastes no time in correcting the thought of this woman and all those present who hear her request. Jesus says that the one who aspires to greatness must serve the rest; whoever wants to rank first must first serve the needs of all. Jesus goes on to say that he as well has come not to be served but to serve, to give his life as a ransom for the many. Jesus is expressing sacrifice and service, two of the primary ingredients of *agape.* Jesus is not looking for something for himself. No, like Jeremiah, his concern is solely on those whom God has given to him. Remember, Jesus said that none given to him would be lost.

Lent is a time when we think of many things, many ways of renewal. Service, ministry to others, sacrifice — these are *agape,* a special form of love to which we are called this day. As we spend this day let us think how we can show greater love, greater *agape* to others. Let us follow the Master, Jesus, our brother, friend and Lord as we walk the Lenten journey this day.

Thursday Week Two
Jeremiah 17:5-10
Luke 16:19-31

Follow
The Signs

If you are not a native to the area, driving in any major city is challenging at best and utter terror at its worst. If you are not accustomed to the normal ways of doing things in a particular area the roads can be a harrowing experience. In some places the posted speed limit may say "35 MPH" but if you are not going 50 you are in jeopardy of having someone crawl up your back. The law says that when you see a yellow light you should slow and prepare to stop. In many places, however, a yellow light is the signal to "put the pedal to the metal," as they say, and race so as to make sure you "make that light." If you are a little late and the signal turns red, that is okay. The important thing is to get where you are going, NOW! In the cities you will see drivers turn right from the left lane and go straight when they are in the left turn lane. If you are going too slow on a one lane road don't be surprised when the driver behind you all of a sudden streaks by you on the right!

When I observe drivers who seem to be rather reckless, I often wonder what it will take to get them to comply with the law. Will another sign such as "Danger" do the trick? Will it take an accident or some other tragedy for people to be more courteous?

Today's Gospel speaks about following the signs which God gives in our lives. Although Luke is not specific, it seems that the rich man, traditionally known as Dives, did not follow the signs provided by God of his presence. The rich man seems to have ignored Abraham, Moses and the ancient prophets. He seems to have even ignored a living sign, Lazarus, the poor beggar, who has been sitting at Dives' front gate. The signs of God were always there, but he chose to ignore them. Because he has failed to heed the signs of the presence of God, he will now live forever in torment. The rich man, realizing his own fate, asks that another sign be sent to his brothers so that they may escape this horrible fate. Abraham says, however, that all the signs are there; another one, even the sign of one rising from the dead, will do no good.

Do we heed the signs which God gives to us along the road of life? Maybe the sign that God is sending you is to drop a certain habit, a difficult situation, or a certain person from your life. Maybe God has provided the sign to take the right fork in the road, where the center and left look so inviting. Maybe the sign given is to place more trust in God and less in human solutions, to let God be our guide.

As we hear in the beautiful imagery of the prophet Jeremiah in the first reading, the signs that lead to God are obvious. As the prophet says, trusting in God nourishes us like the tree whose huge roots have spread in all directions and are now fed by the stream. Even though the rains do not come the tree will continue to be fruitful, its leaves will stay green, for it always has a source of nourishment. The signs that lead away from God are equally clear. Those who choose to trust in human solutions, who seek their strength in the flesh, they will be like the barren bush in the desert, that enjoys no change of season, that stands in a lava waste of desolation.

The signs are there; they always have been. God is all around, in so many powerful, beautiful and subtle ways. Let us open our eyes to the signs of God's presence. Let us trust in God and be guided by the Spirit. Let us be nourished at the banquet table of the Lord, and find eternal life in the process.

Friday Week Two
Genesis 37:2-4, 12-13, 17-28
Matthew 21:33-43, 45-46

Responsibly Building The Kingdom

If you study leadership techniques you will hear the axiom, "You can delegate responsibility but not authority." There is a corollary axiom which is equally important: "It is essential to know right from privilege when exercising responsibility." Knowing these axioms will lead, hopefully, to the construction of more harmonious relationships between those who exercise authority and responsibility and those who are cared for through that same responsibility.

In our readings today we hear of two different stories of the abuse of responsibility which was originally delegated for beneficial reasons. Additionally, the readings speak of the misunderstanding in describing right versus privilege. In the first reading Israel, most often referred to as Jacob in the Hebrew Scriptures, delegates responsibility for the welfare of his youngest child Joseph to his older sons. They are to watch over him as Israel himself would do. The 11 brothers abuse the responsibility their father has bestowed upon them. They have been given a privilege in having responsibility for their younger brother; a right has not been given to them. The older brothers seem to think that their power is absolute, that they may do as they wish. They have no rights to their brother; they have abused the privilege given to them. The older brothers probably think that they have had the last say in this matter. Joseph will certainly die at the hands of the Ishmaelites. But as we all remember from our reading of Genesis, Joseph has the last say. He refuses to hate his brothers, but rather builds them up so that they may live in their adopted land of Egypt. The sons of Israel had the opportunity to use their delegated responsibility wisely; they missed the chance.

The parable of the tenants in today's Gospel is a second story of the abuse of responsibility. The owner of the vineyard leases out the land of his estate; the tenants are given responsibility to properly use it for the betterment of all. The tenants, like the brothers of Joseph, feel they have the right to do whatever they want to do. They do not understand their abuse of the slaves, the son, and even the owner, as a violation of the trust which the proprietor has placed in the tenants.

All authority ultimately comes from God. God has given us, because we are his children, a certain measure of authority and responsibility. All of us, no matter what our status in life, young or old, rich or poor, famous or unknown, have been given a certain amount of responsibility. How are we doing in properly exercising the authority which has been delegated to us? In the family, responsibilities differ, but they are present for each member. Do we cast aside the person, the object, the task as did Joseph's brothers? Do we consider it our right to do what we want in a manner of our own choosing? Do we have a sense of what our responsibility asks of us? In business the responsibilities are different. Does power, responsibility or privilege corrupt us?

The Gospel suggests another way, another avenue to take in our task, our challenge, to be responsible people. Instead of casting aside people, abusing the privilege of responsibility, we can do something positive. As Jesus states that he is the keystone to the structure, so we can make others the keystones that help build the Kingdom of God in our time. We build God's Kingdom each day with what we say and do. We do not have to wait for the Parousia to build the Kingdom. In fact, building the Kingdom is our task, a challenge that can only be accomplished by effectively empowering people to be the cornerstones in our society.

Let us use the responsibility given us wisely. Let us build up the people for whom we have been asked to responsibly act. Let us build the city of God this day!

Saturday Week Two
Micah 7:14-15, 18-20
Luke 15:1-3, 11-32

Be Reconciled
To God

Life is a journey. Like all journeys life has a beginning, a middle and an end. Within the journey of life there are numerous shorter journeys, each of which has a beginning, a middle and an end. One journey within the journey of life which accompanies us along the road is our life of faith. Faith has a beginning, at least in a formal sense, through baptism. The long middle ground of faith is our life, the numerous times we encounter God and find ecstasy and the times when we fail to see or even shut out God. The journey of faith, like the journey of life, has ups and downs. The journey of faith has an end as well: the day of judgment by God.

The Lenten season is a journey, with a beginning, a middle and an end. We have experienced the beginning with Ash Wednesday. We suggested that our spring training had begun; we needed to get prepared. We are now in the middle of that training as the Lenten season progresses. We know that the end of the journey will be celebrated with the great high holy days of the Easter Triduum. Now in the middle of this special journey of faith, we are encouraged by our readings to take seriously still another journey, the journey of reconciliation.

Reconciliation is a journey with various elements. It is a process by which Christians are reunited with God and God's people. Since reconciliation is a process, a journey, there are definite elements which may be identified. Each element is essential to the whole; they feed off one another. If we cannot achieve the first steps, those that follow may not be possible.

The first element of reconciliation is passive, but absolutely necessary to the process. We must believe that God is there for us, ready to welcome us back at any time. In our first reading today, the prophet Micah tells us that God does not persist in anger, but rather, God delights in clemency. God will have compassion on us; God will cast into the depths of the sea all our sins. God will always show faithfulness to his people. God will not give up on any human being. When we know that God's mercy is ours, that God will continually pursue us, as Francis Thompson describes so powerfully in his famous poem "The Hound of Heaven," then we know the journey of reconciliation has begun.

The journey of reconciliation continues with the discovery of the three active aspects of forgiveness, within self, with others, and ultimately with God. The parable of the Prodigal Son which we hear in today's Gospel best illustrates this second step in the journey of reconciliation. Active reconciliation must begin within our own person. The so-called prodigal son comes to the realization that he needs to forgive himself. He has wasted his father's money; he has lived a wayward existence. Before he could begin the physical journey back to his father he needed to find a change of heart within himself. He needed to forgive himself before he would be ready to accept the forgiveness of others.

Reconciliation with others is the second active element. The older son in the parable is representative of one who cannot forgive others. He is angry with his brother because of his wayward actions. He is even more incensed, however, by his father who has not only forgiven the younger man's transgressions, but has celebrated his return with food and dance. We learn about the need to forgive others "through the back door" in the character of the older son. Since this young man cannot forgive, the process of reconciliation is stunted. As when the weak link in the chain snaps and destroys the usefulness of the whole, so too if either of the first two active aspects of reconciliation are not found, the final aspect, reconciliation with God, cannot be achieved.

The forgiving father in the Gospel represents God. His youngest son was barely in sight and the father had the celebration prepared. Reconciliation was achieved as soon as his wayward son realized that he needed to be forgiven, by himself and others. Jesus' arms are outstretched on the cross as a sign of his welcome of us when we have strayed off the path that leads to life. All that is necessary to achieve this reconciliation is for us to ask.

Lent is certainly a time to think about our need for reconciliation. We are given this holy season to prepare ourselves for the Easter Triduum. If we are not reconciled within ourselves, with others and ultimately with God, then the benefit which the Paschal mystery can provide will not be totally ours. We will feel incomplete; we will have lost a great opportunity. Today our readings challenge us to reflect not only on God's mercy for us, but our need to be reconciled with all people. The process begins with self, moves to others and finds its fulfillment in the Lord. Let us this day reflect on our need for healing, our need to be made whole again. Let us continue the Lenten journey in a spirit of reconciliation this day.

Reflections:
Week Three Of Lent

Monday Week Three
2 Kings 5:1-15
Luke 4:24-30

Expectations —
What Should They Be?

Expectations are one of the unavoidable realities of life. Although expectations will differ from person to person and from situation to situation, everyone has certain expectations. This is true in how we view events, material things, specific situations, and especially people. If we are honest, most of the time our expectations are high, especially when it comes to results desired and the usefulness and/or effectiveness of things we need or appropriate. Our highest expectations are found with people and for many the highest expectation is with self.

When our expectations are high this creates a two-edged sword. We look for the best, rather than the worst — this is good, certainly the best way to go. The problem occurs sometimes when our high expectations are not met or things turn out differently than we expected. Then we become disappointed and miss the possibilities and opportunities which are placed before us. Expectations, if we are not careful, can lead to much needless pain and anxiety.

Our readings today speak of unfulfilled expectations, in action and person. In the first reading from 2 Kings, Naaman has convinced himself that the action needed to cure his leprosy must be miraculous in some manner. Certainly no ordinary action could cure such a dreaded disease. Moreover, since the prophet of Israel is quite famous, the actions he performs must be grand so that all can see and, therefore, believe. Naaman is disappointed with Elisha to the point of anger. The prophet did not even come out to Naaman. He only sent word that Naaman should plunge seven times in the Jordan and from this action be cured. Naaman wants a grand sign; he has a preconceived notion of what must happen. Fortunately for Naaman his servants convince him that he should do as Elisha has instructed him. In the process he is cleansed of his leprosy.

From the Gospel it is apparent that the audience in the synagogue was disappointed with Jesus. We know that Jesus was reared in Nazareth. In such a small community it is probable that all those present that day in the synagogue knew him from boyhood. Some of them may have been his companions. The people of Nazareth had expectations of the role of prophet and the role of Jesus. The expectations were not met. Jesus was not what they wanted him to be. Jesus was rejected and he told his sisters and brothers (in so many words) that he was disappointed in their attitude. The people in turn were angered at Jesus' words. They expelled him from the town with the intent of killing him.

Expectations are part of our daily life. Expectations can be very good. We look forward to our vacation; we expect to have a good time. We expect to find some relief from our pain through the doctor's advice and our hopes are fulfilled. Expectations, however, can be destructive when we will accept nothing other than that which we expect. When an idea does not pan out the way it was planned, when a situation does not bring the hoped for result, when a person does not measure up to the standards we have set — then we set ourselves up for disappointment. The problem is not with the idea, the situation or the person; the problem is with our level of expectation. Certainly we can expect a certain level of courtesy from people; we can expect others to be Christian in their attitudes and actions. But we set ourselves up for disappointment, frustration or even anger if our expectations cannot be changed when things don't go as planned.

Accepting people for whom they are, situations for what they bring and ideas for their possibilities in the attitude which will take us where we want to go. It is a good and positive attitude to have high expectations, to want things to go well. This is especially true for ourselves. But if we cannot accept what happens on a day-to-day basis, if we cannot accept others, if we cannot accept ourselves, then we should re-think what expectations we have set and, most especially, our reactions to the reality that we receive, see or feel.

As we spend this day, let us think how we can better accept that which God gives us this day. Some things will go just right; others will not work out at all. If we can accept the people, the situations and the ideas that God sends us this day, then we will be better able to see the presence of God in all things, a vision of the Kingdom now and to eternal life.

Agents Of Reconciliation

Few people today would question the statement that Augustine of Hippo was one of the greatest saints who ever lived. Augustine was a bishop, a great theologian, a prolific writer, and certainly a defender of the faith against the Pelagians and the Donatists. Augustine was a great Christian and through his ministry, life and writings has become the vehicle by which many have come to conversion and greater faith. Augustine, however, only came to his Christian greatness after many trials; he needed a second chance.

Augustine was born in the 4th century to a pagan father and a Christian mother, St. Monica. It was clear from childhood that Augustine was exceedingly bright. In his early years he wandered trying to find himself. He was involved in a relationship which produced a son, Adeodatus. His inquisitive mind led him to become a follower of the Manichaees, a highly rigoristic sect that was popular in the Patristic Church. The group must have had a powerful attraction to interest someone of the stature and intelligence of Augustine.

God, however, had other plans for Augustine. His mother Monica never ceased in her prayers for his conversion. Augustine was lucky; God gave him a second chance to get his life together and make the best of what God had given him. Augustine made good on the second chance. He realized that he had come late to God. As he wrote so beautifully in his autobiography *The Confessions,* "Late have I loved you, O Beauty ever ancient, ever new, late have I loved you. ... I have tasted you, now I hunger and thirst no more." Augustine's second chance became the second chance for many of us who follow his lead.

Our readings today on the Lenten journey speak clearly of forgiveness. They also clearly speak about how God has given us a second, a third, a hundredth chance. Now God asks us to do the same in our relationships with others. When one reads the Hebrew Scriptures the recurring story of God's people falling into and out of favor with God is ever present. Azariah, as a faithful Jew, was aware of the history of his people. In today's First Reading he prays that God will again have mercy on his people. Generation after generation God has been present for the Hebrews and has always forgiven them. The Hebrews have received the second, the third, the hundredth chance from God. Azariah has complete confidence that God will again forgive the people and return them to Israel from their captivity in Babylon. All Azariah can offer God is a contrite heart and a humble spirit. Still, Azariah believes that this is all that God truly wants. God wants a forgiving spirit in our attitude toward others as well.

The confidence which Azariah displays is brought to fruition in the parable of the forgiving king. The king gives the servant a second chance. The debt is written off; it seems that nothing more is required. But as the story continues we see that there is one more very big item that is required — namely the servant must be an agent of forgiveness to others. This he is unable or unwilling to do. Thus, the king has the servant thrown into prison until all the debt is paid.

Each of us knows people who have been given a second chance on life. There are the dramatic stories of people like St. Augustine; there are the simple tales of ordinary people. Each of us in our lives as well have received numerous chances from God. God is true to today's Gospel and has forgiven us seventy times seven times. The question remains for us, have we been as forgiving to others as God has been to us? Have we been agents of reconciliation in a manner similar to how God has treated us? We have all received many opportunities to show forgiveness. Many times, if we are honest, we have not been welcoming to the one who has hurt us. Possibly the pain is still too deep; maybe we are hard of heart and refuse to recognize the sincere sorrow and desire for reconciliation on the part of others. Jesus' warning in the Gospel is a powerful message: "My heavenly Father will treat you in exactly the same way unless each of you forgives his brother from his heart."

Forgiveness is part of Lent; it is part of our spring training. We must seek forgiveness from God and God's people. We must also be ready and willing to extend the hand of reconciliation to others. Let us listen to the challenge to forgive others; let us be agents of reconciliation this day!

Wednesday Week Three
Deuteronomy 4:1, 5-9
Matthew 5:17-19

The Spirit
Of The Law

To a non-lawyer like myself the law seems to have two parts, the letter and the spirit. The letter of the law is what you see, what is printed; there can be no arguments as to what it contains. For example, the United States Constitution states that there are three branches of federal government: executive, legislative and judicial. Furthermore, in the legislative branch there will be two separate houses with representatives elected in a prescribed manner. The spirit of the law is different. For me, the spirit means the intent of the law — what the framers of the Constitution intended when they wrote the document. In the Bill of Rights citizens have been given the right to bear arms. For 18th century society this was not only common, it was necessary for the many daily needs that required such a weapon. Today the need is much different. One might ask: What was the intent of the law? How should it be applied today?

Today in our readings we hear about the law, both the letter and the spirit. The Hebrews were, as we know from our reading of the Old Testament, a people of the law. In fact, the Pentateuch or first five books of the Bible contains 613 laws of greater or lesser importance. The law governed the whole lives of the people. If one followed the law as it was given in the Scriptures, if one followed the letter of the law, then all was fine. A member of the Hebrew community knew if she was in or out by how she conformed to the law as it was written and handed down from generation to generation.

In today's first reading we hear how Moses gave the people the law. They were instructed to observe the law in the new land which God would provide for them. Observance of the law is equated with wisdom and intelligence. Other nations will observe the law of the Hebrews, the law of Israel, and will be amazed. Finally Moses says that the people are to pass on the law to their children.

In the Gospel we hear more about the spirit of the law. We remember from our reading of the Scripture that Jesus was criticized on several occasions for his failure to obey the letter of the law. When he cured on the sabbath or his apostles did not properly purify themselves before eating, they were in violation of the law. The Lord always discounted these incidents. Yet today he says that not one part of the law will be done away with until it all comes true. What does Jesus mean? I think the answer is found in understanding what Jesus means by fulfilling the law. When we hear fulfill we think carry out, but Jesus must mean here that his mission is to bring the law to perfection. Jesus is saying that the letter of the law is only part of the law. The spirit, the intent of the law, is equally important. The spirit of the law for Jesus is submission to God's will. What we are to teach according to the Gospel, "the least significant of these commands," is the perfection and completion of the law, its spirit. The letter of the law is finite, it needs the spirit, the infinite, to be complete.

How can we bring the law to perfection; how can we carry out the spirit of the law? One way would be to release ourselves from slavery to the past. What we learned in past times is good and important, but it need not be the end of our education. Can we broaden out and see ways to bring our knowledge to greater completeness? We need to reflect, to pray and ask, what would Jesus say or do? What is the intent of the government, the Church or the community? How can the letter and the spirit work together to form a more complete understanding?

Vatican II gave us, among other things, a fresh way of looking at the law. As mature Christians we are asked to reflect on the law and God's will in our lives. Let us try to better submit to God's will as we know and understand it. Let us live the intent, the spirit of the law in imitation of Jesus, the one who brings all things to perfection.

Thursday Week Three
Jeremiah 7:23-28
Luke 11:14-23

Union
With God

Unity and disunity, wholeness and division — these terms seem to be self-explanatory. Unity and wholeness are the ideas of being together. Disunity and division are the concepts of being separated. There is more to these concepts, however, that must be understood. Unity is something that is natural in the world. Whether it be atoms seeking other atoms for stability or humans seeking togetherness in community, it is common and normal for unity to be sought and found. Disunity, on the other hand, is not natural to our environment. In general disunity or division is to be avoided.

Since unity is that which is normative we need to look at some models, some images to help us better visualize this idea. One good image of unity in the environment is the concept of alloy metals. Alloys are substances which are compounds consisting of two dissimilar metals. Through a special bonding process the alloy, or resultant metal of the union, is stronger, longer lasting and more durable than either of the two metals from which it is made. Rivers are another example of unity. Tributaries feed into the larger river. The resultant river is wider, deeper and more useful than any of the tributaries from which it is formed. People demonstrate the greatest example of unity. Nations are independent sovereigns, yet it is quite normal for individual nations to be a union of smaller groups. The United States, a union of 50 independent sovereigns is a good example. Nations bind themselves together as well in such organizations as NATO or the Common Market.

The readings today speak of unity as a need in our relationships with God and one another. It seems in both readings that God has been disappointed by the lack of unity in the Hebrew people. In Jeremiah it is clear that God is frustrated with the Hebrews. God has worked untiringly for the people. God rescued the people from bondage in Egypt. The prophets were sent one after the other in order to bring the people to greater faith and unity as a community, as God's people. God's faithfulness has been answered with disobedience. The people have turned their backs on God. The nation of Israel no longer listens to the voice of the Lord.

In the Gospel we hear more frustration, this time on the part of Jesus. The Lord has just healed a dumb man. Additionally, the people are well aware of Jesus' message and his many miracles. Yet he is accused of being in league with Satan and possessed by Beelzebul.

Jesus realizes that there is a need for unity in the community. The ever-wise Jesus says that a house divided against itself cannot stand. Jesus' message is an appeal for greater unity. This unity is two-fold: the people must seek greater unity with God and stronger ties within the Jewish community itself.

Where do we stand in our personal relationship, our unity, with Jesus? Are we waiting for some special sign from heaven, as Jesus says in the Gospel? Are we waiting for some special invitation? Are we estranged from God by our attitude or action? What do we need to bring ourselves closer, in greater union with God?

How are we doing with our relationship with God's people? Have we kept others at a distance? Do we, in word or action, create more discord than harmony? Are we builders of ties that link others or do we break them?

Lent is a time to come to greater harmony, to a greater sense of unity in all aspects of our lives. We must begin with ourselves and settle what may be troubling us inside. We can then make greater efforts in building unity with family, friends and business associates. Lastly, we need to review our relationship with God and see how greater bonds can be forged in this most important of all relationships in our life.

Unity makes us stronger; it is something we as humans need. Let us continue our spring training by seeking greater unity in our lives. Let us reflect upon our need for reconciliation as the Lenten journey continues this day!

Friday Week Three
Hosea 14:2-10
Mark 12:28-34

Love Is The Binding Force

As expressed in yesterday's readings, the concept of unity is very important. Unity is natural to our world; it is that which we seek. In order for things to be united there must be a binding force that keeps them together. Ancient peoples learned the usefulness of combining two metals to produce a third which was more durable and longer lasting than its original component metals. Only recently, however, did scientists discover that the binding force for this third alloy metal was energy. In a unique way energy binds the various atoms together so that the metal which they compose will be the useful product which we need and desire. Human society has its binding forces as well. For those of us who live in a democratic system of government, the law of the land, the Constitution, serves as the binding force. All peoples recognize that this document is the system by which we operate in generating laws which help society to function smoothly. All public officials take an oath that they will uphold the law of the land in their duties.

The binding force for human relationships is more fundamental, yet much more complicated. The basic binding force for us must be love. Love serves as the glue which joins people to one another; it serves as the unifying principle for our relationship with God as well.

Our readings speak about love as a unifying principle for human relationships. The sometimes stormy relationship between God and the Hebrew people is a story of falling into and out of love. God's fealty was always present, but that of the people of Israel sometimes faltered. Hosea preached to the Northern Kingdom of Israel before its capture by the Assyrians. In our reading today the prophet exhorts the people to return to the Lord before it is too late. God, the one who is ever faithful and true, will heal the defection of the people. God will always love them. It is the love of God that allows the relationship to continue despite the periodic faithlessness of the people.

In the Gospel we hear the famous "Golden Rule" of Jesus. We are to love God first with all that we are. We are also to love others as we love ourselves. It is significant that when asked by the scribe to state the "first of all commandments," Jesus gives two laws, bound together with the common theme of love. Certainly Jesus is asking the scribe, and all of us as well, to see that it is impossible to separate the love of God from the love of neighbor. Love must be the binding force in the way we conduct our lives; it must be the glue that keeps us close to God and one another.

Love is a complicated concept — this is nothing new for any of us. Today's readings show that love must be manifest in the respect we have for others. God gave free will to humans, the ability to say yes or no. God does not command love from the Hebrews or from any of us; God has total respect for people, his greatest creation. God lays out the options and allows people to choose their response. Certainly there is a response which leads to life, this is the response of love. As Jesus says to the scribe, "You are not far from the reign of God." As the Lenten journey continues and we seek new ways of unifying ourselves with God and others, let us always remember the need to love as the perfect response to our God who has always loved us!

No Need To Impress God

Making the right impression is something of high value these days. We learn this "necessity" from the earliest times of our life. We need to make the right impression in school so that others will like us. The proper impression is essential if a young person wants to go on a date, anything less will cause much embarrassment. Making the right impression in business is essential as well. We wear the best three-piece suit or the most attractive dress we own for the all-important interview. The more people notice us the greater our chances for the job.

The impression we make upon others, unfortunately, is important in this world. With competition for jobs, schools, programs, almost everything, as strong as it is, a positive impression must be made. Since our competitors will not tell others about us, we need to do it ourselves. How we look, the words we use, the habits we maintain — all of these create an impression upon another. Many times the impression that we give is a false one. The real person lies buried beneath the coating that must surround us so as to appear acceptable to others.

At times the impression we need to make in the world of society carries over to our relationship with God. We think that God will not accept us unless we have done something great or can boast that our name is known by many. We need

71

to remember, however, that God does not ask for our resume when fostering the relationship he has made with us personally. No, God asks nothing other than we be ourselves, the true persons that he created.

Today's Gospel is perfect evidence that God does not care about lofty position or household names. The attitude that one brings is all important to God. The Pharisee is one who wants others to know that he is important. His acts of fasting and payment of the tithe are good actions. Certainly God is pleased with people who sincerely fast or support the Church so that God's work can be furthered in the world. But if one does not engage in such works, that one is no less acceptable. It's the attitude that one takes which matters. The Pharisee is trying to impress God. God, however, is not impressed. God knows the Pharisee; he knows us as well, better than we know ourselves. God knows the heart; he knows our intent.

The tax collector is a sinful man. He is broken and realizes the errors of his life. This man, as Jesus says, went home justified, because he was honest and made no attempt to impress God. Hosea says in the First Reading that there are only two things that God is looking for in us, love and knowledge of God. If we fill ourselves with these ideas then we have all that we need. An attitude of haughtiness, one that tries to make an impression on God, leads nowhere. As Jesus says, "Everyone who exalts himself shall be humbled while he who humbles himself shall be exalted."

The Christian has the tall task of living in the world, but not being of the world. In living in this world it many times becomes necessary to make the right, proper and favorable impression on others. This reality of the world in which we live must not dominate the way we live in our relationships with others. Some of the most humble people have made the greatest impressions. St. Theresa of Lisieux and Mother Teresa of Calcutta are only two of the many examples that we could all name. In our relationships with God and one another the attitude of humility will get us where we want to go. Making a positive impression is important, but it need not mean being who we are not or wish to be.

Lent is a time to seriously consider our relationship with God. The season is dedicated to prayer, fasting, almsgiving and other works that allow us to rethink our need to impress our God as we many times try to impress our world. The world asks us to make a name and seek a position; God, as Hosea says, asks only for love and knowledge. Let us try the humble route confident that God knows our hearts and intent. Let us seek God this day!

Reflections:
Week Four Of Lent

God
Restores Hope

In 1935 Bill W. and Dr. Bob lived on the fringes of society. They were drunks spending their nights and many days drinking away the cares of life. Both men needed someone who could help them to regain their dignity and self-worth. They found that special person in each other. The story of the sobriety and recovery to productivity of these two men is the story of the beginnings of Alcoholics Anonymous (AA), an international organization which over the years has certainly saved the lives of millions. This body of men and women profess that their lives are out of control and need the help of God. AA has served in saving the physical lives of many, but its value has been seen more profoundly in restoring to productivity many who were dead inside, although they may have been physically active. The hope which AA has given to so many has been in a true sense a resurrection from the dead.

Today we hear about the hope that only God can restore to those who have lost the way, to those who may be dead inside. The Hebrew people were certainly a group who had to endure many hardships. Because of their faithlessness to God and God's agents, the prophets, the people were sent into exile in Babylon. While there I am sure they had great difficulty keeping their spirits high. They probably thought God had abandoned them. They may have even felt that they deserved it, after all they had not upheld their end of the covenant.

Yet, in the end the people were returned to Jerusalem and they began to rebuild their lives. In today's First Reading Isaiah speaks about the new Jerusalem. It will be a place where the past is no longer remembered. The new city will be created to be a delight. People will live very long lives; the cries of former days will not be present. The people will live in the houses they build and eat of the fruit of the vineyards they plant.

The renewal of hope which only God can give is illustrated in the Gospel as well. The royal official believed that Jesus could cure his son. He came from Capernaum specifically to ask Jesus to act. The man not only believed; he had complete trust. When Jesus told him that his boy would live, the man left confident that all would be as Jesus had promised. The man's belief and trust were rewarded with the renewed health of his son. Jesus' action is more than a miracle; it is an act of hope. John says that Jesus realized that the people of Galilee would not esteem him. Yet, the Lord returned to the area of his childhood in order to show the people that the only real hope they need must be in him. Jesus' action on behalf of the royal official's son is a sign for all that the hope for which the people have been waiting is present among them; they need only to open their eyes and believe. The royal official has led the way; others must now follow.

During the season of Lent we seek to renew the Christian hope which is an integral part of our life of faith. At times all of us despair for different reasons. We may have had a tragedy in the family, a business failure, or we simply despair about the state of our world. During this period of preparation, our annual spring training, we need to re-think where our hope must always be located. We at times look in other places, but the ultimate hope for our world can only be found in God. Let us, like the people of Alcoholics Anonymous, like the royal official, place our lives in God's hands. The path which Jesus gives will lead to eternal life.

Tuesday Week Four
Ezekiel 47:1-9, 12
John 5:1-3, 5-16

The Greater
Power Of God

Anyone who has had any contact with the sea knows both the power and the life-giving nature of water. When one visits the ocean the power of the sea is easily seen and felt. The surf pounding against the rocks relentlessly pushes against the shore and all that is present on it. People are tossed about like toys as they swim in the surf. On the high seas the power of the sea is even more evident during a storm. Huge waves crash over vessels imperiling the ship and its crew. The ocean with its mighty power can be a frightening place during a storm.

The sea also provides a great deal of life to our world. Many vessels travel over the oceans in bringing goods from one land to another. The waterways as a means of transportation give life to various countries which need the outside support. Island nations such as Japan and Malaysia are totally dependent on the sea for all that comes to them. The ocean also teems with life that we use. Fish provide a great source of food. Plant life, especially kelp, is used in many different applications. The ocean can provide so much for us.

The image of the power and provision of water is brought to mind in today's first reading from the prophet Ezekiel. The Prophet is asked to wade in the water. As it rises he begins to see the power that is present in the stream that becomes a raging river which can only be crossed by swimming. More importantly, the river is a great source of life. The river flows out from the temple of the Lord, the source of life. Wherever the river flows life abounds. The fresh waters of the river provide a place for the fruit trees to blossom on a continuous basis. The fruit of these trees can be used for medicine.

In the Gospel we also hear about the power of water. The Sheep Pool was believed by the Jews to have the ability to heal the sick. The belief was so strong in the community that people flocked there to find relief from their suffering. It is hard to imagine that the man in today's Gospel had been sick for 38 years and yet had never had the opportunity to experience the healing waters of the pool. As John says, Jesus knew that the man had been sick for a long time. Despite the fact that it was the Sabbath, Jesus unhesitatingly cures the man. The waters may be healing but Jesus' power is immediate and greater. The man picks up his mat and walks away, cured of his long-time infirmity.

There are many things in our lives that seem to have both power and the ability to bring us to greater wholeness. We place our trust in the cures and remedies of things and people which bring only temporary relief. Sometimes we seek answers in withdrawal from the world, through chemicals or distance or isolation. The remedies that seem so powerful can do only a limited amount. The world is finite; we cannot ask any more from it. God, however, is infinite, thus all things are possible if we place our trust in the Lord.

The world today is full of temptations which ask us to seek the quick answer to our problems. We look to what is powerful today and hope that this can bring us that which we seek. The truth, however, is that we must seek answers in God, the one who is infinite in our lives. God's solution may not come with the frequency and speed that we desire, but the effect will be fulfilling and permanent. The man at the Sheep Pool did not want to wait to be healed. His situation of forced delay, however, allowed him to experience the permanent healing of body and spirit which is possible with God. Let us today in our reflection and preparation seek the same.

God Cares
For Us

A few years ago I was called to the hospital to visit a woman who had just given birth to a baby boy. The birth was difficult and there was some concern for both mother and child. I had been walking the pregnancy route with this woman so I felt we knew each other well. When I arrived in the room I witnessed a beautiful scene. My friend was holding her little boy tightly to her as she suckled him for the first time. There was an unspoken but nevertheless powerfully communicated act of love being played out before me. The woman was clutching her son and the boy in turn was reaching out with his little hands as if to say, "I am here for you." The mother certainly was the one who would be providing material things for this child, but at this moment both were equally providing love for the other.

To me the whole scene was a miracle. Only two hours earlier this child was in the womb. Now, after the miracle of birth, a little person was before me, clutched in his mother's arms. The miracle of birth was outshone, however, by the miracle of love and caring. The natural bond between mother and child was being manifest in a language of love. At that moment mother and child were one, united in caring and nurturing love for one another.

All of us have witnessed similar scenes between mothers and children. The image is very vivid and this is why Isaiah uses it in today's first reading. The Hebrews in exile needed the reassurance that God was there for them. The prophet says, God will release the prisoners; hunger and thirst will be dispelled. A road will be cut through the mountains; all highways will be made level. It might seem impossible that a mother would forget her child. If she should forget, however, God will never forget Israel.

The oneness that the child and mother experience at the moment of birth is the reality of the relationship between God the Father and Son. Jesus describes the respect and honor that characterize the love of God. As St. John says in his first epistle, "God is love. He who abides in love abides in God and God in him." God is defined as love and thus can be nothing else. God is one, living as a community of Father, Son and Spirit. All that the Father is and possesses is given to the Son.

The love that God shows to us, the care that is our experience of God's presence in our lives, must be shared with others. First we must give back to God the love and caring that is shown to us. The little child cannot do much when compared to the mother, but the reciprocity of feeling and emotion is present. Such must be the way we approach God. We cannot do much compared with God but we can spend time in prayer and reflection with our best friend, the Lord. After we have shown God our love, then we need to pass along that same love to others. We are asked to wipe out the hunger and thirst that others have for God by our attention to them. We are asked to cut through mountains and make highways level. We are asked to care for others as a mother cares for her child, as God has always cared for us.

God is present in what we do and say. Our responsibility to care for others is part of the Christian call to holiness. When we show our solidarity, our oneness with others, in their plight and suffering, we show the face of God to them. The oneness of God which Jesus expresses in the Gospel must be our goal as well, with God and one another. Let us continue the Lenten journey by preparing ourselves to be people of greater care and love. The experience will be fulfilling as we bring the Kingdom to a greater sense of reality in our world.

Accepting
The Lord

The gifts of God are truly innumerable. God has given us the created world and all that is in it. We have the beauty of nature and the usefulness of the world's resources. God has given us one another, for support and love, God has given us our faith and nurtures it along the path of life.

Certain gifts of God separate us from all other living beings. The presence of our soul is the primary gift that only humans possess. Our souls are immortal and thus allow us to live in eternal life with God. God has given us two other gifts which separate us from the rest of God's creation. We have the ability to think and we have free will. Unlike all other animals, humans can think, process ideas, and make decisions. Some decisions are easy, like what clothes we will wear today. Others are more difficult, such as what occupation we will pursue in our lives. Part of this thought process is our free will. We have the ability to say yes or no to all things on any given day. Our yes and no applies in our work and our relationships with others — it also applies to our relationship with God.

Our readings today center on the choice which each human has in relationship with God. The Hebrew people made a choice to build a molten calf. As we remember they went to Aaron and asked him to help them with this project. The Hebrews used their free will to opt for idolatry over God. They knew God; they had just witnessed God's powerful action in their escape from the tyranny of their Egyptian oppressors. Nevertheless, they chose to say no to God. Had not Moses been able to curb God's wrath, the punishment for the people would have been the loss of their chosen-people status.

In the Gospel Jesus speaks of his rejection by the people. Jesus claims that people do not have God in their hearts because they have failed to recognize the Son. He says further that people will accept praise from one another, but they will not believe in nor accept the glory that comes from God. The people have chosen to say no to God's invitation, an invitation to life. Others who come in God's name have been accepted, but not Jesus.

The gift of free will is special. It can be used for many positive purposes. If we wish, society can benefit greatly by what we do. People will profit by our choice, if it is our desire. The power of the gift, however, can be misused as well. As always the choice is ours. Many times the decisions we make are an option for or against God. We are asked to make a choice which means we can accept or reject God, the one who is the source of all good. At other times, as in the First Reading, we make decisions which create false gods. When we opt for power, wealth or prestige at the expense of God, then we have created false gods in our lives. The temptation in our society is great. The common and acceptable thing to do these days is to opt for that which is not of God. We are considered in the mainstream when we go the normative path of society.

Free will allows us to choose the path we will follow. We have the opportunity each day to accept God more fully in our lives. It may be difficult, it may be less acceptable by peers, but to use our free choice to accept God and God's message will, in the end, prove not only courageous but the way that brings us to fulfillment. Let us think this day about how God has called us to use well the gifts we have been given. Let us choose God so that all we do may flower and blossom on Easter morn.

Friday Week Four
Wisdom 2:1, 12-22
John 7:1-2, 10, 25-30

The Challenge
Of Jesus

Challenges enter our lives in many ways. One of the primary ways we are challenged is with our setting of goals. When we are young we set a goal to attend a particular college and thus we encounter the challenge of getting good grades and participating in sufficient extra-curricular activities so that we will be accepted. Athletes many times set goals that create great challenges. One person may set the goal of making a sports team; another may set the higher goal of reaching the Olympics. Each of these goals requires much work and creates challenges.

For me the greatest challenge comes not in goals that we set for ourselves but challenges that come from the outside. When we challenge ourselves it is something we generally want to accomplish; there is a significant amount of motivation on our part to meet the challenge because a reward we desire will be ours. When people on the outside challenge us, however, it generally means that we must change or do something that may not be to our liking. It may even be distasteful.

We are many times challenged by the words and ideals of others. In the 1930s and '40s Mohandas Gandhi challenged the British government to allow home rule in the land of India. Gandhi's ideas and his non-violent method were not popular with many, both in and outside of India. Gandhi's challenge was too great for many. In the 1960s Martin Luther King, Jr., challenged all Americans to truly profess the precepts of the Declaration of Independence, that all people are created equal. Dr. King was controversial; he challenged the sensibilities and moral attitudes of a nation. As with Gandhi, many found Martin Luther King, Jr., too much to handle. In the late 1970s Archbishop Oscar Romero in El Salvador challenged the prevailing attitudes toward the poor and helpless of society. Romero had come from the aristocracy; he was thought by all to be one who would not challenge the system. Yet, the injustice around him was too great; he was forced to speak out. As we know in the cases of all three of these men, the end was an untimely death. The challenges that they provided to the people with whom they had contact were, in the end, too great. For many it is easier to eliminate the source of challenge, rather than subject themselves to change.

Like Gandhi, King and Romero, Jesus was one who challenged the system and the peoples of his day. The First Reading from the Book of Wisdom foreshadows the reaction of people to the life and work of Jesus. Jesus was all too much for the people of his day. He challenged the system and the beliefs of the people to such an extent that he was thought to be obnoxious. As the author of Wisdom says, Jesus, as foreshadowed in Scripture, criticized the people for their actions toward others. Jesus pursued a different path than the people of his day. He was a challenge that the people were not willing to endure. Thus, they speak of besetting the just one, of condemning him to a shameful death. These people knew not the councils of God; they could not discern the innocent soul's reward.

In the Gospel we hear again about the rejection of Jesus. Jesus challenges the authorities who think they know his origins. Jesus' origins are from God, but the people are not willing to accept this. Rather they want to seize him, but as we are told Jesus' hour had not yet come.

How does Jesus challenge us? In what ways are we asked to change so as to find the Lord this day? The challenges of God, like the challenges of life, come to us in many ways.

Maybe we are being challenged to move in a different direction in life. Doors seem to be opening but we are hesitant to investigate let alone enter. Possibly the challenge of God is felt in our need to modify our attitudes and beliefs toward certain issues or toward groups of people. God's challenge may come in the invitation to greater involvement in the local community including the Church.

What is the reaction we give to the challenge of God? Do we ignore the challenge or worse yet become angry and do all we can to rid ourselves of that which asks us to change? This was the reaction of those who secured the death of the Lord. Hopefully our response is more positive. We may not be able today to dive head first into any and every challenge that comes our way. An open attitude, however, is important so that we can grow and in the process find God in ever more great and wonderful ways.

Of all the seasons of the year Lent is the perfect time to attempt to stretch ourselves. We will not be able to do all things, but we can make efforts to broaden who we are. Mohandas Gandhi, Martin Luther King, Jr., and Oscar Romero all accepted challenges to broaden themselves and then had the courage to challenge others. Let us, as our spring training continues, be open to change and to challenge. Let the special presence of God, in its many forms, transform us this day.

Saturday Week Four
Jeremiah 11:18-20
John 7:40-53

Seek
The Truth

We have all heard the expression, "they live on the other side of the tracks." Sometimes in various towns this expression describes a reality, a physical division of the city. In all cases, however, the words "the other side of the tracks" bring to mind certain images. Isolation is one idea. Those who live on the other side of the tracks are isolated; it is best to stay away from these people. The other side of the tracks generally means the bad side; one does not want to be caught on that side. What would people think? A stereotype comes to mind when we think of those on the other side of the tracks. People who live there are poor, many times unruly. They are certainly not of the ilk with whom we choose to associate. Contact with such people will only lead to problems for us.

In his lifetime Jesus was cast in a similar stereotype. In today's Gospel we hear about Jesus as being from Galilee. For Jews of that period, Galilee was the other side of the tracks. Galilee was in the northern half of the country; it had produced nothing of importance for Israel. The Messiah was to come from Bethlehem in Judea, the land of kings and royalty, the land of power and the law.

Yet the people are confused. Jesus seems to come from the wrong area of the country to be a person of any value. The works he accomplishes, however, signify something special about him. His words as well are attractive. Still, Jesus comes from the wrong area; thus he is labeled as one who is unworthy. This person from the other side of the tracks is causing problems for the elite of Judea. Thus, the ruling powers drum up a plot to eliminate him from their midst. Jesus and his message are not to be tolerated.

Jeremiah also knew the rejection of those who could not handle his prophetic message. Jeremiah prophesied to the people of Judah. His message was one of reform so that God's disappointment with the people would not grow worse. Jeremiah decried the injustice done to people by those in charge. The "other side of the tracks" mentality even existed within the confines of Judah itself. As with Jesus the people will not listen; thus they hatch a plot to rid themselves of the voice which challenges their power and way of life. The truth is painful; this makes it unacceptable.

In our contemporary society we stereotype people all the time. We stereotype by ethnicity, race, gender, religion, age and appearance. Certain people, either individuals or groups, become unacceptable to us. Differences in attitude, ways of thought, methods of action are all threatening — they challenge our sensibility. We feel we must rid ourselves of these "thorns in our side." We do all that we can to keep ourselves isolated from the "undesirable element" of life. We sometimes keep people down by destroying their self esteem. We eliminate in so many words those we cannot handle by ignoring their ideas and presence.

Jesus was not a conformist who met the standards and qualifications of those who ran Jewish society. He was outspoken; he was defiant. Jesus was a rebel in many ways. Yet, Jesus professed the truth in all that he said and did.

We can learn from those we consider undesirable or unworthy just as Christ, the one who was not accepted, taught the people of his time. Those resistant to learning new things will miss the opportunity; those open to new possibilities will gain abundantly. Let us reject the prejudice of "the other side of the tracks" mentality which dominates our world. Let us seek the truth and the truth will set us free.

Reflections:
Week Five Of Lent

The God
Of Forgiveness

Humans love to tell stories about others. We tell many humorous stories which bring out the beauty of one's personality. We tell stories of heroism, bravery and significant accomplishments. Sometimes we even hear and tell stories of unconditional love and kindness shown to another. These are the types of stories we like to hear, ones that pick us up and make us feel good.

Humans are far from perfect and thus there are other stories we tell which are not so pleasant. Children are some of the best at telling adults all about the not-so-good things that their brothers and sisters or friends have done. Children love to tell Mom when sister or brother broke a dish or messed up the bathroom. Children love to tell others that someone has done something wrong. Children are known to be good "tattletales." Adults are not free from this scourge of misplaced stories. Sometimes adults talk behind the backs of others because they are afraid to confront the individual personally. We sometimes describe the inadequacies of others in an effort to get ahead. At times, unfortunately, we are cruel and untruthful in what we say. Some people call this character assassination; the Church calls it sin. Accusations abound in our world, few are positive.

Our readings today are filled with accusations, judgments and the problems which exist as a consequence. The two elders of Israel, as described by the author of the Book of Daniel, are guilty on two fronts. They have lusted after Susanna, and then when their efforts are not satisfied they have falsely accused her of inappropriate behavior. The two men are frustrated in their lust and thus out of vengeance make the accusations. In the end their plot is discovered through the wisdom of Daniel. The Law of Moses contained no mercy; rather the elders have exacted on them the penalty they tried to impose on Susanna.

In the Gospel we hear another story of accusation, but there are several important differences. From all indications the accusation against the woman is true. She does not deny it. The law says she is to be stoned, but the Lord goes above the law and offers another alternative. Jesus, the one who is always trying to be a teacher, uses this case to bring forth a great lesson. As St. John says earlier in his Gospel, Jesus came to save, not to judge us. The woman has committed an offense, but so have all those who are her accusers. Some Scripture scholars say that when Jesus bent down and wrote in the sand he was writing down the sins of the woman's accusers. As the scribes and Pharisees looked down possibly they saw their own transgressions against the Law of Moses. According to that law all present should have received punishment, but unlike the Daniel reading all leave without any stripes.

Jesus makes no condemnation of the woman or her accusers. The point here is that God alone is the one to judge, not any of us who walk the human journey each day. It is easy to accuse others; our righteousness sometimes "impels" us to tell someone what others have done. Our need, our frustration at what we know or have observed cannot be satisfied until all is in the open.

All of us in our daily walk of faith encounter similar experiences as those described in today's readings. The accusations will not usually be as graphic or significant, but they are present nonetheless. We accuse people by our words; we make judgments by our attitudes and how we relate to people. We will all find plenty of sinfulness, but as the Scriptures say, take the plank from your own eye before you pull the splinter from the eye of your neighbor.

Jesus would not be trapped by the insensitivity of the Pharisees. Their accusation contained condemnation as well. Jesus is above the righteousness of those who think themselves self-styled and important. Let us take stock of the way we conduct ourselves in our relationships with others. An attitude, a frown, an unkind word can accuse or condemn. Let us take the attitude of reconciliation which Jesus professes in word today and later in deed on Calvary.

Tuesday Week Five
Numbers 21:4-9
John 8:21-30

Seek The Higher Sign

Signs of all different types and meanings are an everyday part of our lives. Some signs give us needed information. You cannot drive very far without seeing many signs which tell the speed limit, directions to reach a certain destination or warning of problems ahead. While you are on the road you will see other informational signs, such as an advertisement for a new movie, a theatrical performance or the latest fad in dress.

Some signs are far more powerful than merely providing information for they raise certain emotions. When one looks at a swastika it is impossible to look away without thinking of the Holocaust and the many other horrors of World War II. Different emotions are generated in us when we see the national flag. It is a sign of the nation, but it stands for so much more. In the flag we see the ideals of democracy and freedom, treasured beliefs in our society.

Religious signs are also very powerful and bring forth much emotion. Catholics use many items which are signs or sacramentals. Things like the Bible, rosary, holy water, statues of the saints and more are examples of religious symbols. Such signs have special and many times different meanings for each person. I think most all would agree that the cross is the best known of all Christian symbols. It is a symbol and an instrument of torture, pain and death, but it also serves, through the paradox of our Christian belief of finding life through death, as a sign of life as well.

Our readings today are dominated by special symbols. The Jews, both in the time of Moses and the time of Jesus, failed to believe in the power of God in their lives. They constantly sought some manifestation of God's presence before they could believe. In the Book of Numbers we hear another incident of the Hebrews' failure to keep faith with God. The author says that the patience of the people was worn out by the long journey. They were not satisfied with the food provided by God. Remember God was the one who provided the manna and the quail in the first place. In punishment God sends serpents which kill many. However, God never abandons the people and sends another sign. The raising of the serpent in the desert prefigures the raising of Christ on the cross. The bronze serpent is a sign of the constant presence of God with the Hebrews.

The faithlessness of the Jews continues in the Gospel. Jesus realizes the people's inability to believe. One more sign will be given. "When you lift up the Son of Man, you will come to realize that I am . . . ." Jesus gives a foreshadowing of his own death. The cross will be the symbol of belief. The cross is also a symbol of obedience, the faithfulness which Jesus shows to the will of the Father.

Signs of God's presence are all around us. There are the physical signs, the sacramentals. There are the signs present in nature. These are important and certainly help us along the journey of faith. But the more important signs are alive and breathing. We must be signs to others of the presence of God. If people do not see the presence of God in us then we are not living the fullness of our Christian call. The presence of God in us should inspire others to greater heights, to a more complete living of the Christian message of love. If people do not see God in the one who claims to be a disciple, then we have retarded God's work; we have inhibited the growth of another.

The task of being a sign of God's presence in this world is a tall order. Yet, Jesus had a much taller order. He was asked by the Father to be raised up on the cross to be the universal symbol of the embracing love of God. Yes, Jesus is God, but he was human as well. He accepted his mission and we are all the benefactors of his obedience. Let us think about the sign value of our lives in what we do and say. Let us pass along Jesus' message of love and peace in our world.

Wednesday Week Five
Daniel 3:14-20, 91-92, 95
John 8:31-42

The Truth
Sets You Free

Death is something that is fearful for many of us. Most people find life pleasant, fulfilling, something we look forward to each day when we awake. Since life is satisfying we do all we can to avoid death. This is only natural and right. God gave us the wonderful gift of our lives. We should use it to its fullest for as long as God gives us to enjoy this existence.

Physical death is something that we do a good job of avoiding. We steer clear of problems; we don't take any unnecessary risks. There is another kind of deadness, that which keeps us from being all that we want to be. This deadness does not allow us to live the fullness of the Christian life. Such deadness is all around us and we do little if anything to avoid it. In this deadness we are prisoners, chained like slaves to the world. We become trapped, bound up, dead in ways that only we and God know.

The Gospel speaks about this non-physical type of deadness that invades our life. Jesus tells the Jews that anyone who is in sin is a slave, held by chains. Such a bondage is not physical, but it is nevertheless a significant hindrance. For many the chains of sin, the chains that link us to this world, are more confining than any physical bondage.

The people of Israel had forgotten their ancestral roots. They had forgotten the belief in God that was handed on to them. The Jews of Jesus' time had forgotten the faith of

99

their ancestors like Shadrach, Meshach and Abednego. These three men had total confidence and trust in God. Because they listened to God's word and refused to honor the gods of their captors they were released from physical death at the hands of the Babylonians.

All of us are chained, bound, in many different ways. Each of us has a certain deadness that desires to be released. Some people are chained to the cares of the world. The things of the world are powerfully attractive and make for a comfortable life. The rat-race of daily life binds other people. People are so busy that they have no time for any spontaneity nor, does it seem time for God. Some people are chained by some burden in life, in our family, at work or in the community which will not release us. Others are caught in some situation which holds them fast and will not let go. The past has imprisoned some, through sin. Many people think no one cares about their chains, that there is no release. There is a way of escape. Jesus says in the Gospel that if we live according to his teaching we will know the truth and the truth will set us free.

The walking dead, those chained in some way, are all around us; we are they. We need to turn our lives over to Christ, the one with the keys to loosen our chains. Let us apply the teachings of Jesus to the deadness which exists in different ways inside each one of us. If we can, then we will know the truth and the truth will set us free.

Thursday Week Five
Genesis 17:3-9
John 8:51-59

Upholding
Our End

Contracts are common fare in today's society. We always seem to be involved in some type of contract. Contracts, as we know, are agreements between at least two parties. Each party agrees to carry out certain items in fulfillment of the contract. People who buy a home use a contract. The builder agrees that the home will be constructed according to the specifications of the plans and that the product will be as advertised. The buyer agrees to pay so much money within a prescribed time in order to move in, occupy and be known as the owner of the home. We all know many other examples of contracts that involve products and/or services in exchange for payment.

A very important contract is that made on the day a couple profess their wedding vows. This contract has nothing to do with money, but everything to do with love. The contract is made with each other. Each promises fealty, love and presence with the other until death. Unfortunately, as we know, this type of contract is having great difficulty these days. There are many reasons, many of which have nothing to do with the commitment which was originally made. The contract was made, however, and needs to be honored as best one can.

In our readings we hear about covenants of fealty which have been unfulfilled. In the Book of Genesis we hear about the contract between God and Abraham. God on his part will provide protection, resources and fealty to Abraham and all

101

his descendants for all time. God will be the God of Abraham and his people; God will never abandon them. The contract, the covenant, has an element for the people as well. God asks the people to remain loyal to God. Abraham and his descendants are to keep God before them at all times. As we know from our reading of the Hebrew Scriptures, this covenant was broken many times.

In the Gospel Jesus offers another covenant, another contract. "I solemnly assure you, if a man is true to my word he shall never see death." Jesus promises eternal life to the one who can remain true and loyal to the Lord's message. Jesus has always been loyal and faithful to the word of his Father. He has been faithful, even before Abraham and God made their covenant together. With such a record of loyalty it is no wonder that Jesus was disappointed in the Jews and in their lack of commitment to his covenant. The Lord calls the people liars because they are not true to God's word, as given to them by Jesus.

All of us encounter contracts in our daily lives. We are probably faithful for the most part to these contracts. We do all that we can to assure that we maintain our contracts for home, car or work position. If we do not, the consequences are drastic and many times swift: loss of home, car or job. We are less prone to forget a contract when it physically affects us, especially in something so basic today as housing, work or transportation.

What about our contract with God — how are we doing on this essential, but sometimes less maintained relationship? Whether we knew it or not, a contract was initiated for us, drawn up one might say, between the Church and each one of us on the day of our baptism. The Church promised to always be faithful. It promised that the baptized would have all the rights and privileges of the sacraments. We in return were asked to participate in the life of the Church, demonstrate fealty, and give service and ministry. How are we upholding our end of the contract? God has asked us additionally to be true to God's word. If we are faithful then, as the Gospel says, we will never see death. Have we been faithful in this covenant as well?

This Lent we made a contract with ourselves to enter into spring training. Have we been faithful to the commitment we made? Have we upheld our end of the bargain? Certainly God has been faithful; God can be nothing else. We have a little over one week to go in our journey. Let us apply ourselves to the task. Let us do our share. God is awaiting our response.

Friday Week Five
Jeremiah 20:10-13
John 10:31-42

Open Your
Heart To God

In the British National Gallery in London hangs a painting that is familiar to many of us. In the scene Jesus is pictured in a garden standing before a door to a small cottage. Jesus is knocking on the door. The scene appears to be normal, but a closer examination reveals one important oddity. The door upon which the Lord is knocking has no handle. The painting is a representation of the popular passage from the Book of Revelation, "Here I stand, knocking at the door. If anyone hears me calling and opens the door, I will enter his house and have supper with him, and he with me." The door to the cottage has no handle because it is the door to our hearts and can only be opened from the inside. Jesus can knock all day and night, but unless we hear and open he will never enter. Jesus wants to come to us, but he will never force himself into our lives.

In our readings today we hear how Jesus came to offer the Jews an invitation into his life. The Lord knocked over and over again on the hearts of the people. Yet in the end Jesus received nothing but abuse and unbelief. In the Gospel Jesus says that the people have no faith in him or in his works. This attitude frustrates the Lord. If the people cannot believe in Jesus, they should certainly be able to believe in what he does, his works. Such magnificent works could only come from God. The people have closed their minds and hearts to Jesus.

We can see, however, a certain sense of openness on the part of the people. The possibility of belief, of openness, is present. In the First Reading the prophet Jeremiah realizes that God can distinguish between the just and the unjust. God will take vengeance on those who reject God, but those who are open, the poor and the needy, will find rescue at the hands of the Lord.

Are we open to God? God invites us to share his life each and every day. Are we listening for the invitation? Do we recognize the call when it comes? Are we open to the possibility of God in our lives? The invitation of God is manifest in many wonderful and varied ways. In our families God may be calling us to a sense of reconciliation. It may be within the immediate family; it may be with someone we only see periodically. Maybe someone is seeking our reconciliation and is knocking on the door of our heart. Are we willing to respond? The invitation of God may come to us in our place of work. Maybe we are being asked to take a different tack with someone who has been problematic in the past. Possibly we are being challenged to find a different, more positive attitude toward another. The challenge of God may be in the community as well. Some friends or neighbors may be knocking on our door seeking our support or assistance in some project or community effort. The community that is Church may also be asking for our response. The request may be to consider a more active life in the parish. Our life of prayer might be challenged to expand our horizons and the different possibilities that exist around us. How can we respond? Can we open ourselves to the presence and possibility of God? Can we open the door and allow God to enter?

Lent is a time to prepare our house for the marvelous events of the Paschal mystery, the passion, death and resurrection of the Lord. Lent is the time the Church has given us to conduct our spring training, our spring cleaning as well. Let us sweep the house of our heart; let us open the door. Let us accept God's invitation this day.

Saturday Week Five
Ezekiel 37:21-28
John 11:45-57

That All May Be One

Community is a popular term these days; we hear it used in so many applications. We speak of the world community. People and governments today are beginning to realize that nations can no longer think of themselves alone; independent thought is no longer useful or prudent. What one nation does affects others. Nations must be conscious of this new reality. We hear today a great deal about the neighborhood community. Many places have set up a neighborhood watch association where all residents make a concerted effort to watch out for the welfare of others, especially against crime which is all too prevalent these days. Neighborhoods many times celebrate as community with "block parties" which are gaining greater popularity. Neighbors as a community celebrate festive days and special occasions. Sports teams for young people are another example of community. Team members, parents and friends are united as a group in their efforts to secure victory and teach sportsmanship. The community of the faithful, our Church, is another important body. We gather at Mass, but there are many other occasions when we gather as well. People gather to read and reflect upon God's word. The faithful gather as a group to celebrate the annual parish carnival or fiesta.

What do all of these examples of community have in common? What is it that community tries to instill in us? For me the answer is that we all need to be one. If we can unite as one in mind, heart and purpose, then the combined efforts of the many produce a synergism which raises all efforts to greater heights and possibilities.

In our readings today we hear how Jesus has come to gather all into one community, a oneness with God. Ezekiel, the prophet in the First Reading, prophesies of a new day for Israel. Never again will there be two nations or a divided kingdom. The people will be restored to their native land with one leader for all. There will be an everlasting covenant of peace; God will dwell with his people. In the end God will make the nation of Israel one.

In the Gospel we see Jesus as the fulfillment of the prophecy of Ezekiel. Jesus came to bring unity to all; Jesus came to gather the scattered children of God. The oneness that Jesus sought within the community of Israel was the same oneness that he enjoyed with the Father. In John's Gospel Jesus has made this quite clear: "That all may be one, as you, Father, are in me and I in you. I pray that they may be one in us, that the world may believe that you have sent me." The Jews, however, were not ready for the unity which Jesus offered. The Gospel indicates that Jesus was making progress in his dream of a oneness in Israel. The Pharisees worried that the nation would not survive the message which Jesus professed time and again. The Pharisees saw no community; they only saw dissension.

Where do we place Jesus in our desire to be one? Is Jesus an obstacle as the Pharisees saw him? Hopefully Jesus plays an integral role in the lives we live. Jesus desires to be one with us, as he is with the Father. The invitation of the Lord is always present; it is our response that is awaited. Let us seek greater unity, greater oneness with God. Let us walk ever closer to the Lord as we prepare to enter Holy Week, the final leg of our spring training in the faith.

Reflections:
Holy Week

Monday Holy Week
Isaiah 42:1-7
John 12:1-11

Following
The Road

All people have a vocation in life. Many times the word vocation is applied to priesthood and religious life alone, but this is far too limiting. All people have a vocation, a road that they will follow in life. Some people will follow the vocation to the single life; most will follow the call to married life and family. Some will follow the invitation to become religious and/or priests. Many people will be wives or husbands who work daily to raise any children granted them by God. Some people will work in offices for their daily eight hours; others will work in the fields. Some people will do work that is service related and others will do work that is more privatized and individualistic. Determining our vocation is a lifelong task. Along the road of our quest the greater task is to be faithful to the path which God lays out for us each day.

Jesus had a vocation as well. It is most probable that he was a carpenter by trade, like his foster-father St. Joseph. But Jesus' vocation, as we all know, was much more. Jesus had a message that was broadcast to all who would listen. None were excluded from this special proclamation of love. Jesus had a mission as well. Jesus came to save all through his own death, the great atonement of God.

I am sure that Jesus had to struggle with his vocation as we must in our daily lives. As time went on, the mission, the vocation of Jesus, became more clear. I am sure that Jesus' long prayer sessions with his Father helped him to know his mission and gave him the strength to carry it out. Since Jesus was human I am certain as well that when he came to realize that his mission would lead to death he probably feared the future. Yet as we hear in today's first reading, the first of the famous "Suffering Servant" passages from the prophet Isaiah, Jesus accepted his vocation, "not crying out, not shouting, not making his voice heard in the street." Jesus accepted his vocation without torment, but with grace. Yes, there was the agony in the garden, but the suffering servant came gently not breaking a bruised reed or quenching a smoldering wick. Jesus, the suffering servant, came to establish peace on the earth. His mission was to open the eyes of the blind, to bring out prisoners, and to bring the light.

Jesus realized his vocation would lead to death. This is why he chides Judas for his remarks toward Mary: "Leave her alone. Let her keep it against the day they prepare me for burial." Jesus did not avoid his ultimate date with death; he willingly accepted death as his vocation in life. Jesus' obedience, even unto death, has brought us to life.

We all have different vocations, but there is one commonality. We have all been called to a life of holiness through our baptismal commitment. This life will be filled with challenges; it will not always be easy to accept the call. The model we have is Jesus. He knew that his message would not be accepted. He knew that his mission would lead to an agonizing death of ignominy on the cross. Yet he fulfilled his mission to the fullest. We as those who follow in his footsteps have become the benefactors of his great act of love. Let us make a greater effort to live the vocation we have been given. In this holiest of Church weeks let us renew the commitment we have made to walk closely in the shadow of Jesus. Let our footprints match his on the way to the cross.

Tuesday Holy Week
Isaiah 49:1-6
John 13:21-33, 36-38

The Darkness
Of Sin

The world lives in a daily contrast of light versus darkness. The light is that which is normally considered desirable. Light brings life. Flowers open their beauty to the light; all plants seek the light for sustenance and growth. The light brings warmth from the rays of the sun. People seek the light for many reasons. The light allows the clear path that we desire to follow to be seen and more easily navigated. In the light we know where we are going. We can see any obstacles that are in front of us and do all that is possible to avoid them. People have no fear in the light; all is open, visible and clear. Good things are done in the light.

Darkness is in many ways the opposite of the light. There is the obvious fact that there is no physical light, but the differences are much greater. Darkness is cold, if not physically at least psychologically. People have a much greater sense of fear in the dark. Today many times people fear to go out at night. The darkness of night brings out a certain sense of danger, whether it be real or imaginary. Evil deeds are done under the cloud of darkness.

Throughout his Gospel, St. John uses the images of light and darkness to convey certain concepts or themes. For John darkness represents sin. In today's Gospel Judas leaves the banquet under the cover of darkness. John puts it succinctly, "It was night." Peter, in the same reading, claims that he will follow the Lord to the point of death. Under the cover of darkness, however, Peter too will falter and fail the Lord.

For St. John and other New Testament writers light refers to Christ and all that he brings to our world. This image is quite vivid in the Hebrew Scriptures as well as demonstrated in the First Reading from the prophet Isaiah. In this second "Suffering Servant" passage we hear of how God will make the servant, the one who is the image of Jesus, the light to the nations. Through the servant of Yahweh salvation will be brought to the ends of the earth.

The web of conspiracy and death about Jesus is almost complete. The night and with it the sin of the world is now upon the Lord in full force. Our lives are part light and part darkness. We are daily challenged to seek the light, the way of God. God protects those in the light; he hides them in his quiver as the imagery of Isaiah describes. The light provides the rewards which only God can give. Darkness, on the other hand, produces the betrayal by Judas and the denial by Peter.

We still have two days more to prepare, to get in shape for the great events of this week. Let us maximize our spring training effort by always seeking the light of truth and goodness. Darkness leads away from God and produces through sin despair and hopelessness. Let us seek the light of Christ, the goodness in this world, today and each day of our lives. If we can then the great promise of God will be ours as well — salvation, our life with God forever.

Wednesday Holy Week
Isaiah 50:4-9
Matthew 26:14-25

Sharing The
Pain Of Others

"Rags, rags! Give me your tired, dirty, old rag and I will give you a new, clean, fresh one. Rags, rags." That was the cry to which I awoke one bright, sunny Friday morning. I sprang from my bed and peered out my second story apartment window. There was the Ragman of our town. He was 6'4" if he was an inch, youthful in appearance and strong of build. I had heard so much about him but never actually seen him. I threw on some clothes, bounded down the stairs and out the front door of my apartment building. I thought, this is my opportunity to see where he goes and what he does. I decided to watch at a distance.

The Ragman pushed his basketful of rags ahead of him. He continued his cry, "Rags, rags. Give me your old, tired, dirty rag and I will give you a fresh, clean, new one. Rags, rags." As the Ragman pushed his basket of rags he came across a young woman who sat on the front porch of her home. Even from a distance I could see that she held a handkerchief. Her face was swollen and her eyes were red. She had been crying. "Please," said the Ragman to the young woman, "give me your old, soiled handkerchief and I will give you a clean, fresh one." The woman looked at the Ragman with a puzzled stare. Yet she agreed to his request. The Ragman pulled out a clean, fresh linen handkerchief. When the woman put the cloth to her face, something wonderful happened. Her face was no longer swollen; her eyes were no longer red. She appeared happy and gay. But when the Ragman put the woman's handkerchief to his face, he began to cry, his eyes turned red and his face began to swell. My amazement at what I was witnessing knew no bounds. And the Ragman continued on.

He pushed his basket of rags ahead of him as he walked through the city streets. He came to the main square and there on a park bench he encountered another woman. She was older and her clothes were dirty and torn. Around her head was a bandage from which blood oozed from a fresh wound. The Ragman said to her, "Please give me that old, dirty bandage and I will give you a new, clean one." The woman looked at the Ragman somewhat with disdain. Yet there was something in what he said or how he said it that attracted her. She took the bandage from her head and replaced it with the fresh one given her. As she placed the bandage on her head, the blood flow stopped. No longer was her face tortured with pain. When the Ragman placed the old bandage on his head, he began to bleed in the same place the woman had been injured. His face took on the look of one in pain. I continued to wonder at what I saw. And the Ragman continued on.

Bleeding and crying the Ragman continued to push his basket of rags. He came upon the local town drunk who was sleeping off his night of frivolity between two buildings in the center of town. The Ragman approached, quietly so as not to disturb the man. He pulled the old blanket from the man and covered him with a new, clean one. He also left a set of new clothes. As the Ragman wrapped the old blanket around him, he began to stagger and stumble as if he were the one who had been drinking. And the Ragman continued on.

The Ragman continued to push his cart, stumbling as he went, leaving a trail of blood and tears. He came to the edge of town. There he encountered someone with whom I was not familiar. He must have been a new person in town. He was an older man with a tattered, old jacket. He had only one arm. "Give me that old coat," said the Ragman, "and I will give you a new, clean one." The man readily agreed, after all he

116

was to get a new coat out of the deal. As the old man put on the new jacket, not one but two arms came through, arms that were strong and youthful. But when the Ragman put on the coat of the old man, only one arm came through. As I watched I could not believe what I saw. And the Ragman continued on.

The Ragman, now with only one arm, bleeding, crying and stumbling, continued to push his basketful of rags. At the end of town he found the local dump. With the remaining strength he possessed he pushed his basket through the gate and up the hill. There in the middle of the garbage dump he lay down to sleep and as he slept he died. From a distance I found safe haven in the front seat of an old abandoned vehicle in the dump. I began to cry, so powerful were the events that I had witnessed. My crying put me to sleep, a deep, restful slumber. The remainder of Friday was lost and Saturday passed without my knowing it. But the next day, Sunday morning, I awoke to the most brilliant light. There before me stood the Ragman. He had a small scar on his head, but both his arms were restored. He was dressed in the most glorious white clothes I have ever seen. Yes, he was the Ragman of our town; he was the Christ.[1]

Walter Wangerin, Jr.'s, powerful story of "The Ragman" is certainly a story of resurrection. It is a totally appropriate story on this day, the great mystery of the Easter Triduum as approaches. The Ragman, the Christ figure, takes on himself the pain and suffering of others. He does this willingly, without payment, without return. In the end he is exulted in resurrection.

In our readings today we hear of Jesus who stands ever ready to accept the pain that others will inflict. Isaiah, in the third of his "Suffering Servant" passages, says that the servant has never rebelled. This is the one who takes the abuse of others, the insults that people hurl at him. He does not shield his face from buffets or spitting. The servant has no fear for he knows that God is his help; he will in the end never be put to shame.

In the Gospel we see the end is near for Jesus. The Lord names his own betrayer, but like the Ragman does nothing to avoid the pain. Rather, he willingly takes on the pain of rejection and treason by one of his chosen twelve. Jesus knew his fate, but he accepted it for he knew, in the end, he would be exalted to the right hand of the Father.

Our lives as followers of Jesus must be led as disciples. Service and ministry are the terms we use today to express the way we must care for those around us. Most people do a pretty good job in meeting the needs of others. The example of Jesus, the Servant of God, challenges us to go further. We are asked to take on the lives, the joys and the pains, of those we serve. This is at best a difficult challenge, but it is one we must embrace. Jesus, the one who took on our lives totally, including all the pain we inflict and share, asks us to walk the remaining journey to Calvary with him. Our spring training for this year is now completed. It is our turn to enter into the celebration of the Paschal Mystery. Let us pick up our cross and aid others with their crosses, sharing their pain. Let us walk Jesus' path of pain which will eventually lead to the place of everlasting glory.

-----

1. Walter Wangerin, Jr., *Ragman And Other Cries Of Faith* (San Francisco: Harper and Row, 1984), pp. 3-6.

Holy Thursday
Exodus 12:1-8, 11-14
1 Corinthians 11:23-26
John 13:1-15

A People
Of Tradition

We are a people of tradition. We celebrate traditions in our families, our society and in our religion as well. In our families we celebrate special days in ways which differ for each group. Each family has its tradition for gathering to celebrate holidays like Christmas and Thanksgiving. Other traditions apply to the ways we celebrate birthdays, anniversaries and other significant events in the life of our family. Society has its traditions as well. We have our system of laws and the courts, a tradition handed down from the framers of the Declaration of Independence and the Constitution. Society celebrates national holidays such as the 4th of July in a prescribed, traditional manner. Traditions are handed on from one generation to another. We keep the tradition alive through our attitudes and actions.

This night throughout the Christian world we enter into the most significant tradition of our faith, the celebrations of the Easter Triduum. We celebrate the Paschal mystery, the passion, death and resurrection of our Lord Jesus Christ. Our readings describe this tradition, beginning with the traditions of our spiritual ancestors, the Jews.

The First Reading from Exodus describes the tradition of the Jews known as Passover. Jews today remember their tradition, their heritage, in the celebration of the seder meal on the occasion of Passover. This solemn remembrance commemorates the action of God in salvation history as he rescued the people from their bondage in Egypt. God, the ever-faithful one, has always been there to rescue the Hebrews, to release them from their bonds. The tradition is significant and is still celebrated with much solemnity.

Christianity certainly has a vast tradition as well. The account of the Last Supper is mentioned in all four Gospels, but only the Synoptics describe the institution of the Eucharist on this date. St. Paul is our other source of what happened that evening. Paul tells us in the Second Reading that he hands on to us what he himself learned. In other words Paul is passing on the tradition. The tradition of the Eucharist continues each day throughout the world. Christians gather to remember what Jesus did for us in his message of love and the actions of his life. We remember his death as well which has become salvific for all of us.

We hear about another tradition in today's Gospel. St. John wants us to know that there is more to the Christian tradition concerning the Last Supper than the Eucharist. We learn in this Gospel of the tradition of service. Jesus initiates a new tradition with his actions at the Last Supper. Jesus washes the feet of his apostles, his closest followers. Furthermore, he tells them and all of us to do the same.

In a society which daily cries out concerning injustice, poverty and crime, how can we answer the call of Jesus to a life of service? The basic answer is that we are asked to wash the feet of others who enter our lives, especially those who exist on the fringes or suffer the most. We wash the feet of others in many ways. The most important way is through service and works of mercy. We need to become the servants of others. The service we render to others should become our tradition. This day let us remember the special traditions we have. Let us endeavor to live the new tradition of service in all that we do and say.

Good Friday
Isaiah 52:13—53:12
Hebrews 4:14-16; 5:7-9
John 18:1—19:42

Why Does The World Suffer?

Why does the world suffer? Why do pain, problems and suffering exist in such abundance? We all believe that God is all good, all love, full of compassion and all powerful. This is how we define God. We believe this to be true. Thus, the question bears repeating, why does our world suffer? Why do wars exist and people die in innocence? Why do people in positions of public trust commit acts that cause others not only to lose faith in the individual, but in the system as well? Why do people fight one another when the only question between them is the color of their skin, their political preference or religious belief?

For me the basic answer to these challenging questions is personal choice, our free will to say yes or no to God at any time in any way. Soren Kierkegaard, the famous 19th century existentialist philosopher and theologian, once wrote, "Faith is a matter of choice, our personal decision in finding God." This personal decision, our free will, is why the world suffers. It is free will that allows the drunk to drive and kill others. It is free will that allows people in public service to break the law and thus lower the integrity of the system. It is free will that places certain members and groups in society on the fringe and does not allow them to participate. Free will moves us closer to or further from God. As Kierkegaard wrote, it is our decision; faith is our choice.

Good Friday is obviously a day when we remember suffering and pain, but it is a day which has much more to offer. We hear of Jesus' suffering, his pain and eventual death in our readings. More importantly, however, we need to ask, "Why did Jesus have to die?" The answer is that Jesus did not have to die; he chose to die, so that we could find life. Jesus' death came about of his own free will.

The First Reading from Isaiah, the fourth of five "Suffering Servant" passages, speaks of the servant's free choice in dying. The appearance of the servant attracted no one. The servant was a person of suffering and pain. As the servant gives his life, the will of God is accomplished through him. The sacrifice of the servant will win pardon for the offenses of others. In the Letter to the Hebrews the author says that through his free will Jesus suffered in order to learn obedience. Jesus chose to become human so that he could better understand all of us.

John's passion narrative describes the ultimate act of faith, of free choice, that Jesus demonstrated for us. Jesus dies for others, for you and me. Unlike the Synoptic versions of the Gospel, St. John sees Jesus' exaltation in his death; the cross becomes his throne. For John, Jesus becomes king on the tree, not in his resurrection. For most all of us this sounds strange — how can greatness and exaltation be shown in death? John's answer seems to be that greatness is shown through free will. Jesus chose to die and through this great action he showed the fullness of love. Through the cross Jesus gained his kingship and life for all of us.

Free will is our gift from God, our ability to say yes or no. Our world suffers; Jesus suffers and dies. Both events happen through free choice. This day, Jesus' crucifixion shows us that free will, which has been used to create so much pain, can lead to good, good leading to love and love leading to salvation. Jesus' example of free will, his example of love, must be our example as well. We might not be able to effect systemic change tomorrow, maybe not even this year. We can begin with ourselves, however, in following Jesus' law of love. Let us use our free will for good; let us use our free will for love. Let us use our free will to sacrifice, to die for others, and in the process be exalted with Jesus to an eternal life with God.

Waiting
With God

"Something strange is happening — there is a great silence on earth today, a great silence and stillness. The whole earth keeps silence because the King is asleep. The earth trembles and is [now] still because the King is asleep. The earth trembles and is still because God has fallen asleep in the flesh and has raised up all who have slept ever since the world began. God has died in the flesh and hell trembles with fear."

So begins an ancient patristic homily on Holy Saturday. It is true there is a stillness in the earth. Something, however, is not right; the quiet is not satisfying. The great events of yesterday somehow still have not been realized. How can God be dead? Jesus died in the flesh; but God is certainly not dead. No, Jesus is making preparations today for something truly glorious, something the world will never believe. How can one rise from the dead? It is not possible, we say. We forget that with God all things are possible.

The earth is in mourning, but not for long. The King is asleep, but the day of our salvation is near at hand. The world will not believe the resurrection from death of the Son of Man, will it believe in our own resurrection? We cannot even imagine what God is planning as he rests waiting for the great Easter morn. As St. Paul has put it so beautifully, "Eye has not seen, ears have not heard, nor has it so much dawned on man what God has prepared for those who love him."

Our spring training is completed for another year. We have walked the journey of Lent, we have made our preparation. Now we await the glory of the Risen Christ to fill our lives with the brilliance which only God can give. Let us spend this day in calmness, but with great anticipation. As the early Christian homily says, God has raised up all who have fallen asleep. The promise of God, the gift of eternal life, will be ours as well.

Easter Sunday
Acts 10:34, 37-43
Colossians 3:1-4
John 20:1-9

He Saw
And Believed

"He saw and believed." These powerful words come from today's Gospel. What do they tell us about the Easter message? The words say and Easter reveals that we must find it in order to believe it.

Hermann Hesse in his wonderful novel *Siddhartha*[1] speaks of the search for life and meaning, a story of seeing and ultimately believing. Siddhartha was the son of a Brahmin or religious holy man in the East. One day he went to his father and asked permission to leave the village of his birth in search of the meaning of life. Initially his father was hesitant to let him go, but the boy pressed his father. Thus the older man allowed his son to leave. Siddhartha and his best friend gathered a few belongings and left the village the next day in search of the meaning of life.

As the boys began their journey they had travelled less than a day's walk from the village when they came upon a vast and wide river. Siddhartha looked upon the water and realized the emptiness which lay before him. Certainly, thought the boy, this river has no meaning. It is so vast yet so empty. The meaning of life cannot be found here. The two boys hired a ferryman to take them to the other shore. On the other side they continued their search.

After a few days of travel the boys came upon a group of ascetics, people who spend much time in prayer and reflection.

Possibly, thought Siddhartha, the meaning of life can be found here. The boys asked permission from the community leader to join and learn the ways of prayer and meditation. The boys stayed for several years, growing from youths to young adults. But after learning the ways of prayer and filling himself with methods of reflection, Siddhartha realized that the meaning of life was not to be found here either. Thus, the two friends moved on again.

After a few more days' journey they came upon a Guru or holy man. They attached themselves to those who followed this man. After a short while, however, Siddhartha knew that the meaning of life for him was not to be found here. His friend, however, found fulfillment, and thus, the two best friends parted company forever.

Siddhartha moved on in his quest to find the meaning of life. He entered a great city. There he found work; there he found love. He lived and worked in the city for many years. He raised a family. Young adulthood turned to maturity and then to old age. Yet, although he had spent the vast majority of his life in the great city, he still had not found the meaning of life.

Thus, as an old man he continues his search. He leaves the city. He walks for a long time and he comes upon a river. It is the same river that he and his best friend had crossed so many years ago, when they first left their home village. The river is still wide and vast; it is still empty. But now Siddhartha looks at the river with new eyes. He realizes that he has spent his whole life trying to find the meaning of life by filling himself up. Now as an old man he comes to the knowledge that the meaning of life has been before him, wherever he was all along. He only needed to empty himself enough in order to see it.

What did John see and thus believe that day? He saw that the tomb was empty. He realized that his life was full, cluttered with many things. For him the question was could he empty himself enough to receive God, the Risen Lord?

We need to ask ourselves the same question. Can we see and believe or are our lives too cluttered to receive God? We are all busy people; we are addicted to many things. Some of us are addicted to work; some are addicted to school. Some people are addicted to pleasure. Some, unfortunately, are addicted to themselves. At times we are so busy that our priorities get messed up. Sometimes our addictions come ahead of our God. It cannot be this way, if we are to see and believe!

We might not feel comfortable doing nothing, just being. It is difficult to accept the moment. However, if we empty ourselves somewhat then we can make room for God and God's works. The reality of Jesus' resurrection is the message of hope for our own resurrection. But our resurrection need not wait until our union with God in eternity. We can begin now by emptying ourselves. If we are empty enough, if we are open, then we have chosen, as St. Paul suggests in today's Second Reading, the higher realm, that which comes from God. We will then be able to find God and in the process perform the works of the Lord, preaching, teaching, good works and healing.

Jesus' resurrection asks us to revive the human spirit deep down inside each one of us. The empty tomb encourages us to be empty enough to be filled with God. Let us today be resurrected; let us empty ourselves. Let us be re-filled with the Lord, so that we too can see and believe!

---

1. Herman Hesse, *Siddhartha* (Bantam Books, 1951).

Reflections:
Feast Days During Lent

February 22 — Chair Of Peter
1 Peter 5:1-4
Matthew 16:13-19

The Example
Of Love

Human beings have the ability to learn in many ways. Through the educational system we spend a great deal of time learning through books and other written sources. Knowledge that others have gained is shared with us through the media of the written word. Knowledge is also gained through listening. We are a highly oral society these days. We listen to the radio, to tapes and to television. Much of what we know comes through our ability to hear.

The greatest way we can learn, I feel, is through observation. Before children are old enough to read one word or understand a coherent sentence, they are learning. They learn by watching and imitation. Why do children have so many common traits and habits with their parents? One reason certainly must be that they observe and do as they see. When we think about how people learn we recognize instantly the importance of example in our lives. If we all learn by observation and example, then it is possible to learn both the right and the wrong ways of doing things. What we do and how we do it is very important, especially for those whom we most influence: family, friends and people with whom we associate regularly. People observe us whether we want it or not.

In celebrating the Chair of Peter we celebrate the office of the Pope. We celebrate the institution, yes, but more importantly, as our readings suggest, we think of the responsibility that his office entails. The tradition of the Church has always held that Peter's profession of faith and Jesus' subsequent commission of him was the beginning of the office of the Papacy. Peter, whether he knew it or chose it, was given an awesome responsibility that day. He was to bind and to loose, but his responsibility was more fundamental. He must have eventually realized what it was, for he wrote about it in our First Reading. Peter writes, "God's flock is in your midst; give it a shepherd's care. Watch over it willingly as God would have you do ... Be examples to the flock."

The example that Peter was to give is our example as well. All who profess the name Christian are pastors in a certain sense. All of us have people for whom we are responsible. The responsibility may be with our family; it may be in the community. Our principal responsibility may be at work. The example that we give to those people who look to us is critical. People will do as they observe; thus the need to act according to the precepts of the Lord is paramount.

The example we give to others has specifics, but is best expressed in the way we live our lives today. We certainly will find numerous opportunities to show the Christian response in a particular situation. This is our good example. More fundamentally, however, we must live our daily lives in such a way that others will want to do what we do. Our attitude is important in this regard. If we are joyful and positive about what we do then people will be attracted. It is especially true, however, that if we are glum and wear a frown in our daily lives, this too is powerfully communicated. We need to carry an attitude and example of love wherever we go. Then, the popular Christian hymn of past days will be fulfilled, "They'll know we are Christians by our love."

As we celebrate the Chair of Peter we celebrate the great responsibility held in the office of the Pope. Let us not forget our own responsibility, our own share in leading the flock. The Christian call is great; let us answer God's challenge this day with an example of love for all!

March 19 — Feast Of St. Joseph
2 Samuel 7:4-5, 12-14, 16
Romans 4:13, 16-18, 22
Matthew 1:16, 18-21, 24

Simple
Faith

The first book I ever read when I began the seminary, Richard McBrien's monumental work *Catholicism,* defined theology, by borrowing from St. Anselm, as "Faith seeking understanding." That simple enough definition is good but it requires one more step to be understood — how do you define faith? Over the years of the seminary I found many definitions, some highly theological and others centered in the practical. The best definition which I have found combines both. It is found in the Letter to the Hebrews, "Faith is confident assurance concerning what we hope for, and conviction about things we do not see." As followers of Jesus we have a mandate to do our best to be people of greater faith, watering the seed planted by God on the day of our baptism.

In celebrating the Feast of St. Joseph, husband to Mary and foster-father of Jesus, we celebrate faith. It is appropriate that today's readings are filled with examples of faith. We hear of the faith that moves mountains and makes headlines. We also hear about faith of which God alone is aware.

King David was an important figure. He was the first king of the united state of Israel. He was the one from whom the lineage of Jesus descends. David's life was one of public visibility, of prestige and power. David expressed the wish to build a great house, a Temple, for God. But as we hear in today's First Reading that was not to be his lot in life. David is asked to have sufficient faith that the house he desires for God will eventually be built. We know that Solomon, his son, was the one to construct the magnificent Temple as the center stage of Jewish worship.

Abraham, of whom St. Paul speaks in today's Second Reading, had great faith. His supreme act of obedience with his son Isaac was his great testimony and test of faith. The faith of Abraham was seen by many. Through the faith of Abraham the Jews came to be a people. We, as inheritors of the Jewish tradition, also benefit from the great faith of this man. Abraham was a leader, a father of a great nation. His faith, as Paul says, was credited to him as justice.

St. Joseph was certainly a man of faith. His faith was manifest in a different way than David and Abraham. Joseph was a simple carpenter. We have no information but it is likely that few people outside of Nazareth, other than family, knew of him. Joseph was not a great leader; he did not make the headlines in the local paper. Joseph had unwavering faith, however. He possessed total trust and confidence in God. As the definition from Hebrews states, he had conviction about that which was not seen. David and Abraham certainly were men of great faith. They had the advantage, however, that when God came to them, there was a human possibility for God's plan to come to completion. Joseph, on the other hand, was asked to accept a virgin conception. He nevertheless unhesitatingly did as God directed him and welcomed Mary into his home.

We are all aware of the great masters of faith and prayer. Jesus is, without question, the premier example for all peoples and all times. We know as well of the expression of simple faith, the proverbial "little lady in the pew." Today we celebrate the latter. Joseph's faith, which affected only his immediate family, nevertheless allowed God's will to be carried out and salvation history to reach its fulfillment. Joseph probably suffered much ridicule over his decision. Yet, his example of simply allowing God to guide him, his example of complete trust, should be our model as well.

Joseph was a simple man, but he possessed an unquestioning and absolute faith. Whether we be great or small, whether we move society by what we do or have little influence, let us imitate the simple faith of Joseph. If we can, we will help bring God's work to perfection today and each day of our lives.

March 25 — Feast Of The Annunciation
Isaiah 7:10-14
Hebrews 10:4-10
Luke 1:26-38

Saying Yes To God

The recently published book titled *All I Really Needed To Know I Learned In Kindergarten* by Robert Fulgham made me stop and reflect about my earliest days. For most of us the last time we were in a kindergarten classroom was when our last child was that age. For some the last time might have been when we ourselves were in kindergarten. If we think back it is correct to say that all we ever needed to know we learned in kindergarten. It was probably in kindergarten that we got our first hard lessons on social contact. We learned that we needed to ask permission to do things. If we needed to go to the bathroom, we asked the teacher. If we wanted to speak in class we raised our hands and were recognized before we spoke. On the playground we learned to share since not everyone could be on the swing or play ball at once. Kindergarten also taught us to be inquisitive and make every effort to learn.

Kindergarten was the place for something equally important; we learned to say yes. Those who have recently been in a classroom of lower primary age children know that when the teacher wants something done all the hands shoot up in an instant. Children at that age are more willing to volunteer. They are probably not aware of all that they may have to do, but they willingly say yes to whatever the teacher asks. They have total confidence that the teacher will only ask something that is possible and good for them.

It is too bad, but the sad reality is that many of the great things we learned in kindergarten are no longer part of us. When we get older we forget our manners and say what we want without asking permission. We forget to share and even tend to be greedy and possessive with what we own. By and large as well, we lose the ability to say yes when we grow older. Life experience tells us that we cannot trust others and thus we shy away from many opportunities which ask for our assent and/or cooperation.

The Annunciation is a celebration of the "yes" that Mary gave to God. As a practicing Jewish woman Mary most assuredly was familiar with the Scriptures that said a Messiah would be sent to save the people. She may have been familiar with the passage we hear in today's First Reading, "a virgin shall be with child, and bear a son, and shall name him Immanuel." Mary was totally surprised at Gabriel's greeting. As familiar as she may have been with the Scriptures, the reality of the angel's greeting could have been nothing other than a shock.

What was Mary's response to this unbelievable invitation? Mary said, "I am the maidservant of the Lord. Let it be done to me as you say." Mary's fiat, her "yes" to God, was total and unconditional. Like the children in the kindergarten classroom, Mary had no idea what her yes would mean and where it would lead. But that was not of ultimate importance to her. Mary had complete confidence and trust in God that all would be done according to God's will. If she were being asked to play a significant role, then she knew that God would give her all that she needed to carry out God's plan. I am sure that Mary had dreams, like we all have dreams in our lives. Probably she expected to live a quiet life in Nazareth with Joseph as her husband and any children that might be born to their union. In a flash Mary made the decision of a lifetime, a decision which changed her whole future, all of her dreams; she never looked back.

Our lives are filled with opportunities to say yes to God. If we are honest many times we choose to say no. Either the timing is wrong, the task seems too difficult or possibly we are just plain not willing to change. God has given us free will, the ability to say yes or no to all God's requests. Saying no is our prerogative, but when we do we miss the opportunity of a lifetime. God comes to us — we can be open and welcome the Lord or we can be closed and God will pass right by. The choice is up to us.

God's will may not be our will at any particular time. We need, however, to think about what our will should be. As the author of the Letter to the Hebrews says to us, the new covenant is to do God's will. Let us today reflect on the mystery of God's love in sending the Son to our world. Let us think about our response to God's call. Let us, as did Mary, say yes to God this day!

www.ingramcontent.com/pod-product-compliance
Lightning Source LLC
Chambersburg PA
CBHW052108090426
42741CB00009B/1726